MY 50 GOLDEN YEARS

Squire & Prince One
10/81

My 50 Golden Years

5 Decades of Golden Retrievers in Vermont and Florida

Dr. Jack Butz

To order additional copies of this book, contact:
Xlibris Corporation
1-888-795-4274
www.Xlibris.com
Orders@Xlibris.com
50585

CONTENTS

Preface 9

Chapter 1 In The Beginning.. 11
Chapter 2 Practice Makes Perfect—Not!!....................... 22
Chapter 3 Out Into the Cruel World............................... 32
Chapter 4 A New Dog House 41
Chapter 5 The Search For Tawny Too (Not Two) 49
Chapter 6 Enter Miss Missy 59
Chapter 7 Tonsils Is A Puppy?? 66
Chapter 8 The Hoof and Mouth Trophy......................... 74
Chapter 9 The Fire of '74 78
Chapter 10 Out of the Ashes 95
Chapter 11 Party Dog.. 112
Chapter 12 A Prince of a Dog 121
Chapter 13 A Cautionary Tale 132
Chapter 14 Heading South 144
Chapter 15 Northward Bound 166
Chapter 16 Not All Is Fun in the Sun 188
Chapter 17 Life Is a Beach 196
Chapter 18 Vermont Calls 204
Chapter 19 Not You (Melanoma) Again! 211

Chapter 20 Full Circle 218
Chapter 21 It's A Good Life............................... 230
Chapter 22 Parker's New Pal.............................. 235
Chapter 23 The Final Curtain 239
Chapter 24 The Answer...................................... 248
Chapter 25 Golden Resume................................ 251

In memory of Dr. and Mrs. James Roberts, formerly of Woodstock, Vermont who were not only in charge of maintaining the health and well being of most of our Golden Retrievers over the years, but who were wonderful friends and lifelong golf partners. These two helped to guide my wife Gwen and me through many difficult times in the lives of our pets, but also gave us the inspiration necessary to provide a wonderful life for our children and ourselves while at the same time serving the community

PREFACE

For generations, the human race has had dogs of all sizes, shapes, colors, abilities and temperament, and each has adapted to the others mode of life. Some dogs work for us, some protect us, some help us overcome disability, some provide companionship, some help us to hunt and some don't do anything much. The one thing that every dog that is not abused, or poorly trained, has in common is the love that it provides to its owners or keepers. A love that is not always reciprocated by the owners. There have always been some humans who have maltreated and abused their canine friends, even to the most recent assault on dogs by some heartless human specimens under the guise of a sport.

Although there are a multitude of different breeds around the world, each one has a following that varies in size from hundreds to millions, depending on the species. For me, and many others, my choice for canine companionship has for fifty years been the Golden Retriever. In "My 50 Golden Years," I have never had a single dog that I wish that I had never met. I have had Goldens that won ribbons in shows, and I have had Goldens that produced more Goldens. Some Goldens created very tense situations that were resolved happily and some did not.

My wife and four children have also been fortunate to experience the lives and loves of the same 50 Golden years. One was even named "Tonsils" because she was born at the same time as one of the children had tonsils removed. Ironic isn't it? "Tonsils in and Tonsils out."

In the story that will unfold before you is a collection of memories and events that highlighted my 50 years of Golden Love from 1956 to 2006. I have also been blessed by 52 years, so far, of another "Golden Love" provided to me by my wonderful wife Gwen, who has also shared our mutual love of Golden Retrievers. Our four children, ages 46-50 have also been similarly blessed.

When our last Golden, Prince Too, died in 2006, my wife commented to me, half-jokingly, "If I were to die today, you (meaning me!) would probably have another blond in here to cook and clean up in no time." I replied, "No, I would just get two more blond Goldens, and they could at least keep the dishes clean and keep me warm in bed." I do not want to live without Golden Retrievers.

CHAPTER 1

In The Beginning

Last year a friend gave me a book for my birthday that told a beautiful story about life with a wonderful Labrador retriever. As I read through the story, it brought back many memories of my canine family that spanned exactly 50 years, from 1956 to 2006. This included 10 to 12 different Golden Retrievers that helped to shape my family life in a way that nothing else could. I concluded that if one successful author could write a good book about one dog, then 11 dogs might provide a story that had the potential to be of great interest to many dog owners as well as those not fortunate enough to have had a canine companion.

After finally graduating from 4 years at the University of Pennsylvania undergraduate school as a Zoology major and 4 years of U. of Pa. Dental School, my wife of one year, Gwen, and I entered into the United States Air Force to begin the practice of Dentistry.

As anyone who has spent that much time in school knows, a book could easily have been written about that experience. My father had died of a heart attack at age 46 and somehow my mother and I were able to get past the first seven years of study without any debt. A feat that cannot be duplicated today as the yearly expense of medical or dental school is now in the range of $50,000 to $60,000 a year. This is one of the reasons that the cost of medical and dental care has soared over the years.

Just after my father died in 1950, I joined the local Broad Street Methodist Church partially because my previous Lutheran Church did not have a basketball team and I loved basketball! An additional benefit provided by the church was a very active Youth Fellowship where young people gathered together every Sunday evening. It was here that I first met my future bride Gwen Kennedy.

In 1955, after what seemed to be an eternity of long and short courtship traveling, I married Gwen, a beautiful blonde of Norwegian descent, and we then started our life living in a 2-room apartment in Philadelphia while I finished my senior year of Dental School. Gwen worked as a secretary for Atlantic Refining Oil Company in the Personnel Department in Philadelphia, and her $72.00 per week salary kept us afloat. I worked at any and all types of work to help out until I graduated, and we joined the Air Force for a 2 year period which was the start of a life of dentistry and a close relationship with the Air Force that was extended as 3 of our 4 children also served 10 or more years in the Air Force, one is now a Colonel and will retire in 3 years.

In October of 1956 we packed up and moved from my mother's home in Upper Darby, Pa. to Burlington, Vermont, Ethan Allen Air Force Base. On the day of my graduation we had found out that we were in a family way, and at the same time were driving merrily along towards the wonderful wilderness of Vermont. We had no idea that this move would be a transition that would take us from "city kids" to "rural bumpkins." When you live most of your life in an urban situation, it takes some time to adapt to the completely different mode of living found in the wide-open spaces.

We were able to find a small house to rent on a quiet road a half-mile from the Base hospital. The property was in a suburb of Burlington which is the largest city in Vermont and contained 35-40,000 inhabitants at that time. The city is located on the eastern side of beautiful Lake Champlain and is only a short ferry ride to Ticonderoga, N.Y. After we had moved our meager furnishings into the tiny dwelling, we were ready and prepared (we thought) to face our first real Vermont winter. Since there was no garage we had no shelter for our little Ford hardtop coupe, and it bravely withstood the snow, ice and temperatures as low as -40F. You really do not know what cold is until you experience 20 or more below zero. Since Gwen was now in the late stages of pregnancy we had to make sure that our little car would start as regular contractions began. I believe that even the auto had some spasms of it's own! One day, as I went to check the car to see if it had the will to start, I noticed that the windows were ice covered as well as the dashboard display. As I tried to turn the ignition key I leaned on the left armrest, and it responded by snapping off the door. (Damn plastic stuff, whatever happened to metal parts?). As the motor made a few weak and futile attempts to turn over, I began to feel a slight sense of anxiety mixed with a measure of dread. The hospital was 8 miles away and obstetrics was not involved in the formal part of my dental education. Newborns don't even have any visible teeth! To make it even worse there wasn't even a dog or a sled in the immediate neighborhood.

My neighbor thoughtfully explained to me, that in temperatures this low, you need to cover the engine with a blanket and attach a headbolt heater to the engine block to keep some heat inside the engine, and it would not hurt to place a light bulb under the hood to gather additional heat.

This was a wonderful solution, as long as I did not take off for the hospital dragging fifty feet of electric extension cords behind the cold, sputtering vehicle. The car did start at the crisis point, so we made it to the hospital on time although it took 3 days for our first-born child, a son named John, to arrive. I wondered why were we in such a hurry to get going? It turned out that starting the car was the least important element in the child birthing process!

While Gwen was in the hospital, I received a phone call from our Base Commander, Colonel Hovde, expressing his desire to replace an inlay that he found on his tongue when arising. For reasons that I don't even understand, even small objects that are loose in the mouth can remain there without being swallowed all night. There were only 2 dentists at the Base Hospital, and I was the one on call most of the time, since I was the junior officer. It was a Sunday and the clinic was very quiet as I met the appreciative "Full Bird," and I was able to replace the gold ingot with no difficulty. This small event worked to my advantage as a week later the Commander asked if I would like to live on the base near the clinic. This made me as a Captain, the only dental officer to ever live in one of the lovely, old 2 story brick duplex homes that circled the parade grounds, at what once was a beautiful Army cavalry base. We would never have been able to afford a mansion such as this on our meager salary. Maybe we could even have more kids!! The grounds of the base were well supplied with very old maple and oak trees, which added to the splendor of the location, particularly during season changes. It is very difficult to duplicate the beauty that the foliage of these magnificent specimens produces in the fall of the year.

Our house was next to the "BOQ" Bachelors Officers Quarters, which added quite a little fun to our normally quiet life. When you put a group of young Air Force officers, most of whom are pilots, into a dormitory-like setting, it is hard to distinguish it from an ongoing Fraternity party! The major difference was, that these guys were putting their lives on the line for their country, and in my 2 years of service there I lost 2 friends whose careers were ended by accidental crashes of Military aircraft. We never hear about these sacrifices that are taken for granted by the general population.

On our first Christmas we packed up our new little boy John, and headed south for Philadelphia, and my Mother's home. I had no way of knowing that this was to be the beginning chapter of my "Fifty Golden Years." and it was already providing us with some very memorable experiences.

As we celebrated Christmas with my sister and her family, she nonchalantly asked me if we had any place in our lives for a puppy? Her brother-in-law had a sideline business of raising Golden Retrievers and happened to have one left. Neither Gwen nor I in 1956 had a clue what a Golden was, and so, partly out of curiosity we ventured out to Jack's farm outside of Philadelphia. At the time my sister Peg had a very handsome Irish Setter that in color resembled a Golden, but in no way had the calm demeanor that is an admirable trait of most retrievers. Most of the early Golden Retrievers were a darker shade of red than those that dominate the Westminster Dog Show of today. A large number of present day Goldens are very light, and some even almost appear white.

We arrived at the farm, and Jack brought out the male 8 week old (or so) puppy for us to examine. We had no idea that this loveable fur ball would be the genesis of "My Fifty Golden Years," and how this event would change our lives in such a positive way forever. It took us only a few minutes to decide that he had to be our first 4-legged baby and he would make a perfect buddy for our newborn. I gave Jack the $50.00 fee that he requested even though I thought that it was incredibly high, but I did not want to create a family dispute. Jack presented us with the puppy's AKC papers, the ones with all of the fancy names and since he had a color that I referred to as tawny, we named him "Tawny" and drove back to complete our Christmas holiday. With the family gathered around, we were proudly displaying our new little reddish blonde baby boy, but found that most of those attending seemed to be having more fun with our cuddly new pup. I must admit that I didn't blame them because all little babies' look the same don't they, and everyone loves Goldens, especially new little ones.

We headed back to Vermont, with our little car quite overloaded with gifts, and our 2 new precious possessions, John and Tawny. When we went into the house, I had to set up my movie camera in order to record this historical event. As I was clicking away at John who was sitting in the middle of the floor, Tawny headed for John, whom I am sure that he regarded as a new toy, and since the dog was far more stable he promptly bowled the baby over and precipitated a crying spell that was well documented by the camera and might even have been a candidate for a TV home video show. I think that the puppy that was happily licking little John's face was in fact frightening the little guy even more. When Gwen arrived home from the grocery store, and was able to see the first movie production of the result of all her hard labor, she quietly suggested that I should pay more attention to the plight of the baby, who was after all the star of the show, not the puppy.

As Tawny grew to be a very handsome young pup, the Officers next door who always seemed to be sitting on their porch drinking beer, began to notice that he loved to chase a ball. Even though puppies seem to be inexhaustible, it wasn't long before Tawny was pooped, and the guys were entertained. It was then, that the young pilots asked me a question that 50 years later no one would ever ask, "boy he is sure a beautiful dog, what kind of dog is he?" I think that you would have to either be in the Antarctic, or in the jungles of Borneo to ever hear that inquiry today. Nearly everyone recognizes a Golden today. I think that Goldens appear more regularly in magazine and TV commercials than any other breed of dog. They seem to all possess a very attractive reddish-golden lustrous coat with a long feathered tail that acts as a rudder when they are in a full running mode. Tawny, as most Goldens, had a very appealing gentleness in his demeanor and a very expressive beautiful face. It is very easy to become quickly attached to this fantastic array of positive qualities.

As Tawny grew, and John became an "ankle biter," we soon found we were expecting a second child. This child was a daughter Deborah Louise who happily was born in June, a time when our car was quite capable of starting up immediately. This time Gwen was not as ready to rush into the hospital to stay for a few days awaiting the birth, so we waited until contractions became fairly severe and then dashed off to the Maternity clinic. By this time I was beginning to have contractions of my own as I drove speedily along the highway with one eye on her heaving tummy and the other on the road. When we arrived at the hospital, my somewhat "bulbous blonde," looked at me as we started up the front steps, and stated that she could proceed unaided no longer. I promptly dropped the suitcase to the ground, picked her up in my arms, and proceeded through the entrance. I must have been on an adrenalin rush myself because even though I prided myself as being a fairly strong fellow, lifting a fully loaded pregnant woman and carrying her up the steps and into the lobby was not an easy task. An aide immediately put her into a wheelchair and whisked her off towards an elevator with only a brief attempt at a wave. From past performance, I decided that there was no hurry, so I went to telephone her Mom and Dad in New York. After providing the anxious grandparents with the few details that I had at that moment, I proceeded to casually take the elevator to the maternity ward, and when I arrived there a nurse told me that we had a new baby girl. At first I didn't think that she could be speaking to me because I had just arrived on the scene! It took only 41 minutes to deliver, much to Gwen's relief and mine, and I was grateful that I didn't have to work my way through a traffic jam as might have been the case had we lived in New York, where her parents wanted us to settle. There is a reason for everything.

Another milestone passed, but did this mean that I could have another 4-legged friend or keep the status quo? It was decided that the present ratio of one animal per family would be appropriate for now. We had only been at Ethan Allen AFB for a year and a half, and had been blessed by 2 babies and a Golden. Life was surely sweet!

In my 2-year stay at the Dental Clinic on the base, most of the time was spent on routine dental care. I do, however, have a sense of humor, some call it twisted, though not in my eyes, and I just want to recall for you 3 incidents that bring a chuckle to me even now 50 years later. Now that we were settled into our first real home, with our two babies and first Golden Retriever, I started to work on my initial collection of patients. I did say, "work" didn't I, not practice, as so many jokes about Doctors always emphasize. If they only knew! It takes a lot of practice to learn how to practice!

Ethan Allen AFB in Burlington, Vermont was a small Air Force Base that was a part of the Eastern US Air Defense Command. It had been originally called Fort Ethan Allen and was an Army Cavalry base where once a large number of stables, made of brick were made into Offices and storage areas. About 20 two-story brick homes, some of which were single and the rest duplex were situated in a semicircular drive along the periphery of a large parade ground area. This area was a natural playground for children and an excellent spot to hurl objects so that a fast growing puppy could keep himself in top condition. It also served as an area for dog training courses that were held by the watchdog company at the base. The parade ground was surrounded by trees and was beautifully manicured, much like a golf course. We also used it as a golf practice area. This was where I really got my love for golf started. This was the perfect location for a novice golfer to learn, without fearing for someone's safety. However I never took the opportunity to teach Tawny the basic fundamentals of golf ball retrieval 101, and he never really cared about chasing a silly little golf ball. Maybe I should have learned a lesson from him!

Very few parades were ever held by the Air Force, but you could visualize what a spectacular area it must have been in the 30's and 40's, when it was covered with cavalry soldiers and their magnificent horses. They probably even played polo there. It was a wonderful place to live and work, as there was no traffic and my clinic was one hundred yards from my house. The property was of course also gated with armed Air Police lads. The children could not have had a better environment to start life in. It was an Air Defense Command Base with a squadron of delta-winged F-102 Supersonic fighter jets, and was very exciting for a young member of the hospital staff. We had 3 MD's. 2 Dentists and 1 Veterinarian on the Staff there. There was an X-Ray unit and a full laboratory for both the Medical and the Dental Sections. We even had a dozen beds that were seldom used as we had a great arrangement with the local civilian Hospital. The veterinarian was there to take care of the guard dog group, and in his spare time, he treated our personal pets. Most of the personnel on the base were young, and many of them were married with families, which kept us very close as a group, and we have maintained a number of those friendships over the years to this day. All in all it was a perfect place to start a young family. We even made some money, which had been in short supply up to that point. In 1956 I was paid $9000.00 a year but was offered free housing, plus the ability to purchase food and other necessities of life at a reduced price at our Base commissary.

CHAPTER 2

Practice Makes Perfect—Not!!

One snowy day, Jack, the Vet from Michigan asked the 2 MD's from Brooklyn and me if we might enjoy a day of skiing at world famous ski resort Stowe, Vermont. It was located only about one hour away in the beautiful Green Mountains. A famous place to some, but we had no clue what it was, since Jack was the only one of us to ever have skis attached to our lower extremities. The 3 of us brave fools went to the base gym and were fitted, (if that is the operative word!) with skis and boots. The airman who assisted us knew even less than we did about the entire skiing process! The boots were tie-ups and very heavy so as to keep our feet on the ground. (Didn't work!!) The skis were 7 feet long and 6 inches wide, all painted white, probably to cover the bloodstains of earlier heroes. They were undoubtedly left over from the WW II and would have made better firewood than rapid transit objects. We figured that they would probably burn better after we split them up a bit! We left early in the morning so that no one would see us skipping off from working, in the small convertible that belonged to our Vet. buddy, a.k.a. ski instructor. If the Air Force had only known that 2/3's of its hospital staff was on such a dangerous mission as this, they would not have been pleased, but it was important to keep up the morale of the troops. However, we were sure that we would conquer this mountain without casualties, and after all, we did have our own medical staff on site. We all had a cup of coffee at the base lodge, and should have had a supplemental shot of brandy, but what did we know, eh? We didn't even have crash helmets or GPS equipment.

Fortunately, we were the only humans in sight as we approached awkwardly, stepping on each other's white planks as we reached a moving rope with metal objects attached, none resembling a chair. This rope contraption was moving along at an astounding rate of speed, which blurred the image that I was seeing through my ski goggles. Our Vet said that all we needed to do was aim our skis up the hill and grab onto the L shaped metal bar that was attached to the long, moving rope. Seemed simple enough, and after falling off several times, we 3 finally all got a hold on the rope, and like ducks in a row, slithered up the slippery slope with nervous laughter, as our instructor called out to us with encouraging words. All went well until near the top, and then one by one the skis disappeared as if falling off of the earth! I thought they said that the "earth was round?" What happened next was Charlie Chaplinesq. As each one reached the top, we had no idea that a short steep slope downward was the end of the line and nobody told us. As each one crashed to the ground, another fell on top of him until the hysterically laughing instructor ordered us to get up and on our maple slats and either go back down the hill or use the lift rope to lynch him on the spot.

We were, of course, on the easiest and widest slope that could be found at a ski area anywhere, but it did have a solitary telephone pole in the middle of it, and each of us was sure that we would run directly into it. We, of course, did not even know how to stop except to fall. None of us were orthopedists and we didn't even have a first aid kit!

One of the two Brooklyn MD's was a balding Italian, who decided to be the first one to follow our instructor down the hill. Before he could get started forward, he began to slowly slide backwards with great balance, and no control. It was to be his longest vertical trip of the day, as he crashed backwards into some small fir trees. By this time it was impossible for the two of us left at the edge of what appeared to be Mt. Everest, to stop laughing at Dr. Joe, who was now emerging from the trees all covered with snow. He, of course, was very embarrassed, but he need not be, since Mike and I had not even started. The fun was just beginning!

Over the next 30 minutes we took turns sliding, tumbling and slipping down the hill, only restricted by a forward pitch between the big white sticks attached to us or by falling directly backwards. The Lord was kind to us despite a series of epithets that only could be uttered by 2 gents brought up in Brooklyn.

Skiing is not too big in beautiful downtown New York, but things may change when global cooling takes place!

The Vet, of course, watched all of this with pity and encouraging words as we reached the bottom. We were able to go at it a few more times, and almost began to improve to the level of a 3-year-old snow bunny. Our instructor did however, have a treat for us as we sat at the small lodge at the base of the hill. He ordered some coffee and promptly poured from a brandy bottle, that he had not told us about, a proper portion of distilled tranquilizer in liquid form. The next time that we skied there would be a much larger supply of 80 proof liquid!

We left there to return to base with a solemn promise never to discuss the event with our hospital staff. They all wanted to hear all about the gory details! We didn't keep that promise long and decided we would try it again, but never did.

The other two events occurred in my small three-chair office in the Dental section of the Hospital. I had a Senior Dentist who was a Major that went home to Massachusetts to work weekends in a practice that he shared with his brother so that I was always available on weekends for emergencies. In exchange for this accommodation, he would be responsible for early morning sick call so that I could have a good breakfast with my wife, two children and Tawny.

Since I was on duty on weekends, I was approached by the wife of the Base supply Officer Major Davis. Normally we were instructed not to perform dental work on dependants of our

Officers and enlisted men, but we usually had ample time to do some work, on occasion. Mrs. Davis was a charming southern lady from Atlanta and I was happy to be of assistance. She had a full upper denture that did not fit properly and wondered if I would reline it for her. A reline is a fairly simple process that requires an impression and lab work that keeps the patient temporarily toothless.

At first I was surprised that such a lovely lady of her age was a denture wearer, but in dentistry nothing surprises you after a while. I took the impression and advised her that it would be ready the next morning. She was very happy that it wouldn't take any longer since she did not have an extra one. Since I was aware that this nice lady had a great sense of humor also, I decided to have a little fun with her.

We had our own small lab adjacent to the office so that I did not have to send it out to an outside laboratory. Before I relined the denture, I poured a plaster model of it so that I could fashion a temporary plastic acrylic denture we used to call a flipper. Instead of setting the teeth into a normal attractive alignment, I took eight denture front teeth that were extra ones we kept on hand for single replacements, and set the various teeth in a haphazard fashion, which included non-matching colors and strange angles. The acrylic base that the teeth were attached to would fit her upper palate fairly well so that she could wear it at least temporarily. She certainly would not want to wear it very long! Although, I have seen people in the Mall for whom these teeth would have been an improvement.

If you remember the facial appearance of Mortimer Snerd from Charlie McCarthy days, then you would recognize the look that this lady was about to experience. I then proceeded to reline her original denture, and left the office on Friday night with a slight chuckle, in anticipation of what I would enjoy the next morning. The devil made me do it!! I had already decided that I probably would not make a career out of the Military anyway and this would be the last nail in the coffin. In actuality, Gwen and I both loved the Air Force and still do. In the morning, Mrs. Davis was waiting anxiously for me at the Clinic. The hospital was never very busy on the weekend, but someone always had to be there in case of a medical or dental emergency. This was not a trauma case yet, but it had the potential to become one! As we chatted she made herself comfortable in the dental chair and I could tell that she was a little bit nervous, but I was quite used to that. She wondered how her newly lined denture would feel, since it is difficult to be without your teeth even for one night.

I explained to her that the teeth might feel a little funny at first but that she would quickly adapt to the new sensation, and she would return to her original ex Miss Georgia appearance. I don't think that she quite fell for that line, but she was willing to play along. Since I was sitting slightly behind her at the chair, she was not able to see the denture as I brought out the newly fabricated "party plate" as I later named it. As I placed the teeth in her mouth, she said that they really did feel different, a lot different, a whole lot different!! I tried to keep a straight face as I reached for a mirror, so that she could see how good she looked even though the feeling was unusual. I told her that the mouth makes some small natural changes in shape when you leave the old denture out for a day. She looked a bit uncertain as she reached for the mirror to see for herself. It was a good thing that the clinic was closed that Saturday morning, because the ensuing shriek would have emptied the building, and I would have ended up in the "Slammer."

Looking at her unusual countenance as if all were normal, I said. "How does that look?" She could hardly talk as she ran her finger across the misshapen front teeth, all of which were out of line, as if she was a hockey player after an extremely rough game. As I started to laugh she said more sedately "you bastard, these aren't really mine are they?" I replied that yes they are yours, but I have a better set for you. Then she started laughing uncontrollably as she went to look again at the mirror. After we settled down she said how did you do that? " In order to prevent a heart attack, I placed the original denture into her mouth and she relaxed while we both returned to normal, whatever that is. Then she said, "you must let me take these to the next woman's bridge meeting and I will report back to you." We had agreed to keep our little secret for now. She left the clinic a very happy lady who was now prepared to have some fun of her own with husband and friends.

The second fun moment occurred during a normal visit in the clinic. I had a wonderful chair assistant, Tech Sergeant John Powers, who was a native Vermont lad and we became good friends over the two years that I served there. Sergeant Powers seated the patient, a young man who was new to the Air Force, and who was very nervous. As a dentist in the 50s, I was aware, and knew that most patients are very apprehensive because of past experiences of their own, or stories that they had heard from others. At any rate, John and I were in a mischievous mood that day, and decided to have some fun with this nice unsuspecting lad. After examining the chap, I pronounced to John that it looked like we may have to remove the right upper molar, and that it could be a difficult job. The poor airman, knowing that he was not in charge, reluctantly accepted his fate while he prayed to himself for some kind of heavenly intervention in the form of an earthquake.

I told John that we might have to blow this baby out of there! The boy did not know what to do, so he sat there like a good soldier. In Dentistry, a material used for temporary fillings for 100 years known as "gutta percha" comes in the form of pink rods that resembled birthday cake candles. It is normally heated so that it is pliable and is used for a temporary filling. In the lab I took one of the cylinders about two inches long, and attached a 10-inch dental floss fuse to one end of it, making it appear like a small pink stick of dynamite. I told him that this was a new development in surgery, and the material was called Denta-Dyn, and that it would usually work. After letting the lad get a quick glimpse of the dynamite stick, I placed it under his upper lip with the floss fuse hanging down onto his cheek, and while the wide eyed Airman looked at us suspiciously, I asked John for a match and to be sure the area was "clear". Beads of perspiration appeared on his forehead, and as we used to say as kids "the young man didn't know whether to S—or go blind!" What a horrible saying but it did fit the situation. Before I could apply the match to the floss fuse, John and I could no longer refrain from breaking out in wild laughter that was soon joined by the patient. With much relief on his face he said "you really did get me there, Sir!" I shook his hand and thanked him for being such a good sport and promised much more responsible treatment from then on. I handed him the small IED device and asked him to keep it in a safe place. It was a good thing that I wasn't leaning over or he might have considered my butt as a good place to put his newly acquired faux bomb!! He left, and probably thought me to be a little weird, but how could that be, when I love Golden Retrievers so!!

In our last winter at Ethan Allen, our small staff decided to try ice fishing, which is very popular during Vermont's long winters. After finding enough volunteers we assembled a plywood fishing mansion back behind the hospital, and soon had it ready to be delivered to Lake Champlain that was five miles west of us. While hammering and sawing this Codfish condo, we neglected to think about how to place it on the frozen lake. Finally one of the lab technicians suggested that we use our ambulance, which normally saw little or no service on our small base. With some difficulty we hoisted the plywood five by eight shanty onto the roof of the ambulance, and proceeded to drive, without sirens, and lights through the city to the lake. It was a good thing that we did not have an accident because it would have been very difficult to explain to the police what that structure was doing on the top of a military vehicle. I suppose that I could have told him that it was actually a mobile control tower for our small planes, but I don't think that would have flown, so to speak.

We considered that since this was not exactly a "line of duty" event, that we should keep things quiet. All went well as we arrived at the ice and slid the crude structure onto the frozen lake out to a distance of about 100 yards, where other shacks were lined up already. Tawny, the fish retriever, had as good a chance to catch a fish as we novices, but we went ahead and drilled two large holes in the eight-inch thick ice. While the dog peered down into the frigid water, and probably wondered if there were "catfish" down there, we began to sit and drop our lines through the holes. Well, the cold temperature made this adventure lose its appeal in less than two hours, and we packed up and didn't return for several weeks. When we did return, the ice had started to melt, and our shanty was ready to float away, but even a retriever wasn't going in that water, so we watched it disappear, to maybe end up as somebody's duck hunting blind downstream. This episode reminded me of the old Vermont fishing story that goes like this. An old Vermonter was asked how he was able to catch so many fish through the ice? He explained that it took a can of peas and a large hammer. You take the peas and line them up in a circle around the hole in the ice. Then when the fish comes to take a pee, you hit it on the head with the hammer!

CHAPTER 3

Out Into the Cruel World

The time had come to leave the warmth and relative tranquility of our "small town" like military facility. We would miss the occasional powerful sounds of the F-102 fighter jets roaring overhead, and see their magnificent ascent into space. It made you proud to know that you were a part of this essential element of the United States military. I was offered an opportunity to take a ride in one of the special 2-seater F-102's, but declined after I found out that my "Fly Boys,"(who also had a sense of humor) liked to take medical and dental personnel for a short flight to see how we held up during combat conditions. This was one puppy that wasn't going to fall for that ploy, however as I look back upon it now, I probably should have taken them up on it. It would have been an experience that I am sure that I would never get again in my lifetime. My Air Force Colonel son told me that his initial flight in a newer F-16 fighter plane was perhaps the biggest thrill of his entire life!

This flight meant flying in an inverted position sometimes going straight up or coming straight down, rolling from side to side and flipping over. It sounded like fun and I really regretted not doing it, but I was leaving the Air Force with a family, and I would not have any chance to return the favor at the next dental visit. I think the combat pilots had much more fear of a dental appointment than of any foreign foe. My decision to renege was fortified, when a short time before I left the base, one of my pilot friends was flying a training Jet on a mission, along with a supersonic F-102, when they accidentally had a midair collision. Both planes were destroyed, but my friend was able to eject from his cockpit, and parachute to the ground, where he was later found by a search group. He had broken his neck upon impact on the ground and he died there, after having survived the air-to-air collision. Fortunately, we don't have that happen often, but once in awhile is often enough. We just don't give enough credit to these heroic men and women who give their lives to protect this country, and this is especially true today!

As a parting gesture, we did enjoy a squadron farewell party at the small hospital, that was attended by the other medical officers and the technicians who helped us run the facility. One of the advantages that a small hospital had in the military was that certain forms of alcohol were always kept in our inventory of drugs, sealed in a closet. Once a month, one of our group of doctors was required to check the medications and file a report. Ethanol and methanol are found, and used in hospitals quite a bit. Ethanol is the one that is safe to ingest in moderate amounts.

We always had enough extra on supply for patient needs as well as a punch bowl additive whenever the staff had a special party. And all of this time everybody thought that this was only really a good substitute for automobile fuel!

A few months prior to leaving the Air Force, we piled the tiny kids and their furry friend and guardian Tawny, into our two door Ford in order to investigate the potential sites for our civilian practice. I had been attending Vermont State dental meetings and found a few good leads. Gwen and I both knew that we were not interested in living and working near our old home areas in New York, or Pennsylvania, after having lived in Vermont for two years. We were smitten with the idea of living sans traffic and congestion, and were sure that the children and dogs would have a safer and better life in the country. I was just lucky enough to be able to make a decent living, and to surround my little family with a great environment, even with its frigid winters!

I came across a dentist from Woodstock, Vermont, who was about to start a new Orthodontic practice in another town. He recommended that we investigate the area since it was a beautiful example of a picturesque Vermont village. We had already realized that the culture and sheer beauty of Vermont was extremely inviting. At the time there was a small group of affluent folks in Woodstock that were backing the formation of a Health Center for the town of 3000 or so, which could also serve neighboring small towns. They had found a young physician Dr. Hugh Hermann, and needed a dentist to start up this new clinic. At that time Vermont had a human population of 350,000 and an animal count of approximately 360,000 (mostly cows). Since I had never worked on any cow-like critters, I was not too impressed with the large number of four legged milk containers, however, it did mean that there must also be a large number of farmers, most of whom had real teeth! This proved to be true, and I enjoyed having a wonderful experience with hundreds of farm families from as far away as 50 miles! Unfortunately, there are no longer as many dairy farms left in Vermont as the land is gobbled up by developers, and the farm work is too difficult to attract many young folks these days.

Gwen and I had a meeting with the local building committee and found out that they would furnish me with a dental office fully equipped that could be paid off over ten years with no interest. I became very interested since we were living on our military income of nine thousand dollars per year, and unable to accumulate any thing resembling a nest egg. This fact, along with the cost of raising two children and a now larger Golden dog, made us seriously consider this offer. We took a poll, and the affirmative nods of the children's heads and a happy tail wag from Tawny sealed the deal. We had made a commitment that would provide our family and pets with immeasurable joy and pleasure for the next 50 years.

Now we had to consult our respective parents, none of which had ever heard of Vermont. With comments like "Where the hell is Woodstock?" and "we will never see you again," being uttered by the in-laws, we concluded that they needed to see the area, so we invited them to come up and meet us in Vermont, so that they could see for themselves what we were in for. Of course, we had already decided on our plan of action, but it would be nice if they agreed to it.

Two weeks later, when Gwen's parents arrived, we took them to see our prospective working place and the small house that we had picked out that was available for the princely sum of 13 thousand dollars. They were still very doubtful, even after we showed them the two story white Colonial house that stood proudly behind a picket fence that included a one-half acre of land with a nice old red barn, but no garage. Our first real home of our own, and we were very excited and happy, as were the kids and their buddy, Tawny.

The house was in the village itself, and my office was only one half of a mile away. Amidst their protests and statements like "you will be sorry to bury yourself way up here!", we were finally able to at least get them to let us try it, and find out for ourselves. Again the children nodded and Tawny wagged his tail.

As we were getting a little better at parenthood, and the practice was going well, our little foursome was about to become a quintet, with the arrival of Bradley Garrett, a second son that made me feel a little better about the fact that I was the last male member of the Butz family, and we needed more assurance that the family name would continue. Unfortunately, in the present state of the world, there is not a lot of concern about whether a family name perpetuates, or whether one bears any name he or she desires, because the parents are not married anyway. This is a very sad situation, and one that I have endeavored to reverse. All four of our children are married, and as of now have 11 more young examples of what we consider the "right way" to establish a family. Unfortunately ethics, morals, responsibility and common sense are almost becoming impossible traits to find in the upcoming generation.

Just before I got serious about looking for land to build our new home, Gwen came down with a serious case of viral meningitis, which at first was difficult to diagnose, and not easy to treat. As she was in bed with little mobility, she exhibited her wonderful ability to cope with adversity, with no sign of resigning herself to being a cripple. Her mental strength far surpassed her physical strength, but she was sure that she would overcome this scary situation. But with her attitude and some invaluable help from God, friends and neighbors, we were able to survive these months of adversity. It was surely strength from God that enabled the three children to survive Dad's cooking. It was quite fortunate that my office was only a few blocks away, and I was able to get home at lunchtime. Although she was unable to get out of bed, the children, though small, were able to be of great assistance in a house with two floors. It was a few weeks before Gwen was able to get out of bed, and her recovery was remarkable. Because of her young age and excellent health overall, she was able to return to her normal life with no encumbrances. I am not sure what normal is meant to be, because less than a year later our 3rd son arrived. We were well on our way to having at least a basketball team, as Jim arrived and our lives were now very busy with 4 children in 6 years. This was a feat that Gwen's Dad, when he heard the news, remarked "Don't they ever go out??" I wonder what he meant by that?

Over the next two years we had a wonderful time even in the winter, as the children loved the snow that sometimes reached a depth of 24 inches. Tawny did not understand what the snow was, and found it difficult to find the ball or rock that we threw for him to retrieve. They invariably sunk in the snow, but they don't call them "retrievers" for nothing! Tawny had a particular affinity for rock retrieval, and sometimes they were almost too heavy to pick up. I was very proud to show a visiting friend how I could toss a rock off the large stone porch behind the house, out into the black night, and have it dropped at my feet with a "Clunk" within a minute, even though Tawny had not seen where it landed. I learned firsthand why Goldens, and other retrievers, are used around the world to sniff out and find explosives, drugs, and especially live or dead bodies under very difficult circumstances and conditions. The breed has the ability to scent objects that is said to be hundreds and thousands of times more sensitive than a humans'. This fact was proven to me on two occasions by Tawny.

The first time was when we took him to a small local lake that was populated by many family "second home" camps. The water was crystal clear, and the bottom mostly made up of a multitude of various size rocks. When I threw an unidentifiable rock 20 or 30 feet out into the water, that was a foot deep, it was reclaimed in the jaws of this happy, soggy dog in a minute or so. Sometimes he had to come up for air and then duck under again, but he always came back with the right rock. Could he smell it under water or was he just lucky? I believe it was the former.

The second event came later in the same year, and was made possible by the presence of a group of telephone company workers that had dug a trench in the middle of our street, in front of the house. The ditch was about four feet deep as the cables needed to be below the frost line, which in Vermont can be four feet deep in winter. The men were mostly leaning down or kneeling at the bottom, so as to lay the lines. Just before lunch, a knock was heard at the front door, and when I opened the door one of the phone men said to me "is that Big Red dog out there yours?" He seemed perturbed, but I know that Goldens do not attack postmen or pole climbers, and I admitted to him that "yes he was mine, what has he done?" I asked him with a smile. He told me the men had been having fun throwing rocks that they'd dug up in the trench for him to retrieve. The problem was that the men had to stop playing "rock ball" with him, so that they could get their work done. But Tawny kept picking up sizable rocks and dropping them back into the ditch, sometimes landing on the head of the unprepared worker. Even with their safety helmets on, it was proving to be a potentially dangerous situation. We both laughed as I went out to retrieve my playful retriever. I am sure that Tawny was as sad as the workers were glad, that the trench was finished two days later. There will be two more occasions that different Goldens also demonstrated this marvelous sense of smell that I will relate later.

Now that we were settled into living and working in Woodstock, we found out through a magazine article that it was listed as one of the "most beautiful small towns in America," at the time in 1960. Dogs of all kinds were to be found in this wonderful place, and when an AKC sponsored dog show was held there in 1960, we decided to enter our "Big red boy" "into his first show. He proceeded to win a blue-ribbon, but I did not know whether to attribute that honor to his quality or because there were not a lot of Goldens around in those days. That would change "big time" over the next thirty years as their popularity grew fast, and with good reason!

It was in this same time frame that I first was introduced to a man and his wife who were to become our most loved and trusted friends. Dr. Jim and Dot Roberts ran the Woodstock Veterinary Clinic, just north of downtown Woodstock. We established a professional relationship where we treated each other's families for over thirty years. Our friendship was solidified as we found out that we were all somewhat addicted to golf, even though golf is only played in Vermont for about 6-7 months a year, we were able to leave our respective busy professional lives for winter golf vacations, and to establish the now locally famous traditional golf tournament called the "Hoof and Mouth" trophy. Dr. Jim, of course was known as the "hoof" and Dr. Jack as the "mouth."

CHAPTER 4

A New Dog House

Even though we thoroughly enjoyed our little house in the village, we were realizing that with a new addition to the family on his way, that we needed a lot more room. Through a friend in town, I learned about a seven-acre parcel of land, just a mile from the center of the village, which was for sale for five thousand dollars. This was a "Kings Ransom" at the time, but we all have to take chances sometime. At the time, I was earning a little less than ten thousand dollars a year, but this location was too good to turn down, and the thought of a new house with acreage for the dog and children was making the decision easy.

The 7-acre lot was completely wooded with pine, birch, maple, and elm trees. Since the pines were more numerous than the others, the home site would be named "Pine View." The whole family would drive up to the hill known as "Church Hill" often, to watch the progress of earth moving and tree cutting. It was only about 2 miles out of town and was an easy walk if the weather did not allow good driving. Every time a tree fell however, it left Tawny with one less target for his 3-legged stance. This fact was overcome by the massive collection of rocks, large and small, that was uncovered by the bulldozers. He really didn't know where to start looking for his next granite play toy. We placed the cellar hole in the middle of the lot with plenty of land on all sides, and a wonderful view to the west. You could look out of any window and have a beautiful vista of either the mountains or the wooded hills.

I enjoyed building things like most dentists, and with the help of "Better Homes" magazines, I designed the house of our dreams. We used no architect as my builder Max Boynton preferred not to have one. Max was a contractor, who learned his trade from several older Vermont builders, and he had no use for any kind of blue prints, and in the end he built the house mostly with drawings that I had made myself. As of now the house is 48 years old, and it is still one of the nicer homes in Woodstock. If anything was not right, he would take full responsibility for it, and did a wonderful job. We built the house for 32 dollars per foot, which compared to costs of present-day building was a minor miracle. The costs were based on a 15 percent charge over material costs, and there was no set contract price. The job was accepted with a mutual handshake, which was the way things were done in Vermont in the decade of the 60s. How we do miss those days!

At the time, we didn't think a garage was in the budget, so we built without one, but did provide a space for it to be added later. As it turned out it would have been better not to build a garage at all!

The house was a two story colonial building with a brick veneered front, and a full basement, which I built in myself later to add recreational room. You needed a good deal of family room with dogs and children on board, especially in Vermont, with its severe winters. There was a long driveway, since we had seven acres, and it had a 35-foot circle near the house that was tree filled, and made a wonderful split rail fenced in area where the dog could have his insulated house with plenty of tree trunks to water. When it got too cold, or had so much snow as to cover the doghouse we kept Tawny inside, but he was outside too. Dr. Jim said he was healthier outside anyway, as his coat would grow much heavier and make him even more regal. He was now a solid 70-pound dog and probably could have pulled a small sled with the kids sitting on it, but we did not have any kind of harness that would accomplish the job.

The house progressed nicely through the late summer, and when fall approached, we began to visualize what a beautiful vista that we had, which was magnified by the superb color changes that are typical of a Vermont fall foliage season.

As the snow started to cover the landscape, I started the first of my many building projects, using the excess lumber from the house construction. I built an eight by 12 foot Garden house with two windows that sat on the hill overlooking the house. It took me three years to realize that the shed was a little too far from the house, and a soon to be built garage. Because of its size and weight I had to cut it into two pieces with a chainsaw, and with the aid of my trusty new little red Jeep, I was able to move it a distance of 250 feet over the snow covered slippery terrain. Once there, I was able to reattach the sections and the silly little shed rests there now 50 years later. It was now the Christmas season, and the house was completed the day before Christmas. What a marvelous gift for the family that year! Even Tawny had a lovely new abode to enjoy as he pranced around the property with a brand new red neckerchief that was tied around his neck.

Woodstock and Vermont in general are spectacularly beautiful in the wintertime, especially when decorated by Christmas lights. The small village of Woodstock was often used during the Christmas season as the location for several movies and commercial films. Budweiser, in particular, used the surrounding area for several long running ads that are shown in December even today. This year Tawny was fitted with a satin red bow instead of his usual neckwear. This bow was similar to the orange one that we put on him during the Vermont deer season, which was two weeks before Thanksgiving. There were always scores of hunters on or near our property and unfortunately all of them were not good stewards of the hunting ethics.

One year, a frustrated Vermont farmer actually painted the word "COW" on some of his herd after some fool accidentally killed one of the grazing cows during the deer season. Even with a great deal of pressure from "down country" hunters, the

Vermont Legislature has so far resisted the attempts at creating a legal Cow Season! However, since horses bear a striking resemblance to Moose, they may have to be painted orange in the future!

Unlike children in many parts of the country, Vermont children and their families very often have to find their own Christmas tree in the wild forest. Since we had a nice red Jeep, and felt as though we could plow through anything, including two-three feet of snow in order to reach our planned destination. Because of our mobility in rough terrain, we were enabled to take all of the kids and Tawny off to find our own Christmas tree. Many of my patients lived on farms, and were kind enough to offer us our pick of trees on their property to decorate our new home. This tree hunt sounds like sheer pleasure, however with a large dog and several children, to go out in near zero temperatures and tramp around a frozen countryside looking for the "perfect" tree does not always result in one of life's memorable moments. Little voices arising from their bundled, partially snow covered, bodies asking questions like "can we go home now, I am freezing?" and "do we have to do this or can we have some hot chocolate?" There was even a comment from an unknown source that quietly mentioned that there were some real trees for sale at the Church parking lot in town. But in the melee, Tawny was having a terrific time following tracks and scents of deer and bunnies, which were really abundant, and he was in no hurry to return home. But we surged on, since this was a "bonding" adventure, or so we thought, and I know that the children remember it fondly.

When we finally selected the one that was acceptable to all, we piled the snow-laden spruce, fir or whatever it was, onto the top of the Jeep and tied it securely. There was a chorus of happy voices exclaiming, "good job Dad, let's go!" Then we drove through the beautiful heavy white canopy of snow along some of the same trails that countless deer used when they were not being chased. Even though the children had a few frozen tears on their little cherub like faces, we did consider the venture worthwhile, and a learning experience. When we arrived home, the tree had to be placed in the garage so that the frozen snow had a chance to melt. Then the family started to rout through a multitude of boxes, most of which were labeled "Christmas decorations. These "goodies" included many articles that had been passed down through generations, and even had a new stocking with "Tawny" embroidered on it. There is a special scent associated with Christmas that accompanies each storage box, even after they have been closed up in the attic all year. Dad, of course was in charge of setting up the Christmas train setup that seemed to grow larger each year. I had started my love of trains when I was still in college and had a very large "HO" train layout that covered 1/3 rd of the basement and had an abundance of plaster mountains. These heavy plaster hills made it impossible to move the whole setup when I moved out and it was still there for several years. I did take the track and trains with me when I entered the Military and I still have them to this day with the intent to set them up again for one of the grandchildren.

The village of Woodstock has a special fascination of its own, and even had two full-length Hollywood movies filmed there. It was interesting to be able to see and talk with real life film stars like Bing Crosby, Melvin Douglas, and many others that walked our streets for a few months. The snow that often makes it difficult to get to work each day, also made it possible to have large horse drawn sleighs driven by local farmers through the town, especially at night. It was quite a sight to see 2-4 large horses blowing large puffs of what appeared to be steam from their nostrils, as they crunched their specially designed horseshoes through the hard packed snow.

Behind each wagon driver sat an excited group of adults and children, all wrapped up with colorful woolen coats and earmuffs that matched their scarves. Their exclamations of "Merry Christmas," rang through the frosty air, and was in tune with the jingle of small bells that were attached to each leather horse collar. Oftentimes the sleighs would then be guided up a narrow curving road onto the small mountain that borders the village, that is called Mount Tom. At the peak of which there is a beautiful lighted 40-foot wooden star, which was donated by a local resident. The star is lighted for the entire Christmas season, and overlooks the whole town. It is such a serene location that several of my friends have had their ashes spread there after their demise. It is a beautiful and reverent site. In the summer the star is designed such that it can be lighted as a cross during the Lenten Season and can be seen for miles away.

It was shortly after our Christmas, that we noticed that Tawny was having trouble with his digestion of food, and since we had not had any previous experience with a dog medical dilemma, we had to call my user friendly Veterinarian, Dr. "Hoof" Roberts. At first we had to rule out if he had swallowed something which did not qualify as dog food, or whether it was a blockage that was caused by another more sinister cause. As Jim examined him further, he could tell by palpation that there were areas that were probably cancerous tumors, and an X-ray confirmed that fact. I can still remember watching quietly as Dr. Jim's gentle hands moved over the beautiful golden body on his examining table. The look in Dr. Jim's eyes told me that this would not end up happily, and Tawny looked up at us with his beautiful brown eyes, wondering what was happening to him. I felt so helpless since I knew that there was nothing that could return him to his normal life, even with the best of care, and Jim said that dogs often hide their pain. This was going to be the end of the first chapter of my "50 Golden years," but I knew that somehow there would be more.

We had no choice but to euthanize him, and it was of course difficult, but Jim helped make it easier and had the facilities behind the clinic so that he could cremate him there. We lost him in 1966.

CHAPTER 5

The Search For Tawny Too (Not Two)

Now that we had a taste of what it was like to have a Golden Retriever, we knew that we must replace Tawny with another male and call him Tawny Too. A male was preferred at this time, because we already were thinking ahead, and would like a good one so that we could consider using him as a stud, as well as a ferocious guardian of our country property.

As we had come upon our first Golden rather by luck, we decided to look a little deeper into the history and development of the Golden Retriever breed, since it did not have anywhere near the recognition in the 50s that it has now. There is hardly a catalog mailed out to the U.S. population that hasn't had a beautiful Golden pup or some adult featured in its advertisements. There are also, of course, several movie pictures that starred the Golden as the premier soccer or basketball playing canine hero. However, even before all of that notoriety, we had decided that this was "our kind of dog."

Goldens are beautiful, intelligent, loving, good natured, gentle, well behaved, easy to train, loyal, playful, happy, examples of what to look for in a family canine member. Did I forget anything?? I should have more human acquaintances with all of those wonderful personality traits!

Most agree that Golden Retrievers were developed in Scotland and England in the late Eighteen hundreds. In Inverness, Scotland, Lord Tweedmouth wished to develop a dog that had many qualities. He wanted a dog that was loyal, yet energetic, and was able to perform retrieving acts in the water at various temperatures. He was also interested in an animal that was aesthetically beautiful. Sounds to me like a Golden doesn't it? Several dogs of the Spaniel type, a Newfoundland and Irish Setters were all in the mix. The first two Goldens that we had were obviously related to the noble looking Irish Setter with their lustrous dark red coats. Although the majority of Goldens as they are shown and seen on the advertisements seemed to be getting more and more on the cream and light golden color. I always preferred to have them on the reddish golden side even though I could always fall in love with a lighter dog, as long as it was a Golden Retriever.

The Golden has always been known for its ability to be trained, and has been used by many thousands of sightless folks, to ease their difficulties with mobility. Their keen sense of smell has made them well used in the search and rescue efforts of police and fire departments. There have been reported cases of them having the ability to actually scent cancers on humans, in particular, skin cancer, and some have even been able to detect when a life-threatening seizure may be coming upon their master. Their work in drug detection and "Bomb Sniffing" is also well documented. Who could forget the beautiful photo taken during the 911 catastrophe, that showed an exhausted New York fireman kneeling on the ground, head down with his arm wrapped around a handsome Golden Retriever, wearing his official Orange harness, who was sitting next to him as a pillar of strength

There is no kinder, gentler animal in the world that I have ever seen, and every child should be exposed to their demeanor in any situation, and could learn a valuable lesson from them. They are almost too human to be believed, and in many cases maybe that statement might be demeaning to the breed. They are better than a large percentage of humans that I have met in my life. The first three dogs to win the AKC obedience championships were all you know whom -Goldens of course!

Golden Retrievers were granted separate breed status in 1913, and first classified as the retriever (Black, Yellow and Golden) in 1920. They are ranked in the top three of America's most popular dogs, although if you have ever owned one I am sure that there's no doubt in your mind, which dog is America's No. 1. No offense to the lovely labs, oodles of poodles and all of the other nice breeds. There are times when I watch a Westminster Dog Show that I see some critters that make me wonder if they are all really in the realm of Dogdom?? Although many of the different dog handlers that I have observed bear a strange resemblance to the various critters that they are leading around the arena on a string, you can't tell me that those poodles were born with those haircuts!

There is a wonderful institution called "Golden Retriever Rescue Education and Training," or just "GRREAT." This is a non-profit volunteer organization dedicated to the rescue and placement of Goldens around the country. The dogs are sometimes strays, and most often neglected by their owners, some of who cannot afford the care of a pet. The local dog pounds turned over their Goldens to GRREAT rather than euthanizing them. Most of these dogs are adults, and at least partially trained, which makes it easier for a foster home placement. It is difficult to imagine anyone intelligent enough to purchase a Golden in the first place, would be able to mistreat and abandon the same dog. However, we do see that same behavior that some people exhibit with their own children. This organization performs a wonderful service that provides equal parts of joy and love to new owners and the dogs as well.

Meanwhile, as the house was finished, there was much to be done on the yard area. A farmer friend let me use his farm tractor to prepare the land around the house that would support a nice lawn. Since we had 7 acres that could be developed for the future use of the 4 children and their friends human and canine, it made perfect sense to provide a safe area that would keep the kids close to home. It was fairly simple to learn how to drive the machine, and not until I nearly tipped the John Deere over on a steep hill, did I finally understand how dangerous they could be. This was before roll bars were invented to protect the drivers.

Now that I had the area smoothed and contoured, I saw that the surface was dotted with a million small stones and pebbles. It would take me years to rake them up, and for some reason, the children were always busy when I asked for volunteers. They did, however offer a plan that I couldn't refuse, namely that they would do the job of rock eradication on a piece-by-piece basis. I knew then that we had some potential union negotiators living under my roof, concealed as little kids. But the price was too exorbitant, and I had to refuse, with the caveat that if all of the funds derived from their labors would go directly into an education fund, I might agree. A friend told me that our nearby County Prison had low risk prisoners that could be hired to clean up the area, and remove the tiny boulders. This worked out beautifully, especially when I decided to enlarge the area to more than an acre. In two days the entire job was completed by five hard working inmates, (in this case outmates), and I was able to proceed with my farmer act of planting grass seed and later fertilizer. We now had the proper play area for dogs and children. Now to find the right dog!

In order to know where to look in our quest for "Tawny" Too, as our next puppy would be called, we inquired at an AKC sponsored dog show that was held in Woodstock, our new hometown. The name of "Finderne Kennels," in a small town in southern Vermont, near Londonderry, came up as a good possibility. It turns out that the breeder happened to also be the Secretary of the Golden Retriever Club of New England, and she with her husband, ran a renowned kennel. We called them and were granted an appointment with Mrs. Hargraves to be interviewed, so that we may be able to prove ourselves appropriate new owners of one of her babies. It was easier to get one of our kids into an Ivy League college than it was to convince this fine women that we were worthy custodians, however it was well worthwhile.

We left the kennel with a new sweet smelling fuzz ball, with male attachments, and I felt that I had to virtually snatch him from her motherly arms. We were given a list of instructions and rules that made the ones given to us after our last child's delivery seem puny. It was easy to see that this lady was very sincere, and we knew immediately that we had a small four-footed treasure in the fold. After all, the pup had better papers than we did, and we came from fairly decent heritage. The children were overjoyed with their new possession, as were we all. The drive through the beautiful Vermont Mountains and valleys was indeed one filled with gratitude and happiness.

It took us quite awhile to live by the rules that the kennel provided us, and I can see why this lady was secretary of AKC. Her meticulous attention to detail was why her dogs were such good examples of what results when you pay heed to proper training regimen.

Tawny Too proceeded to develop exactly as she had forecast, and when he grew to 65 pounds, we went through a prescribed "dog training" class with varied results. When he received his degree of "Summa Cum Again," it was mutually agreed between Dog Professor and I, that maybe a little more training should be in Tawny's immediate future. He was voted best-looking Golden in the class, and did not have any nervous accidents on the gym floor. The fact that he was the only Golden in the class was later found out to be the explanation for his new "Title." We were soon to find out that raising a young dog also has some tense and scary moments, to make up for the pleasant experiences.

We were preparing for a short vacation that would include children and canine companion. As we looked around the house for Tawny Too, to no avail, we received a phone call from a neighbor who was only one-quarter mile up the road. Larry asked us if our dog was home, since he and his wife had just finished performing a dog rescue operation in their own semi-frozen pond. They were in the process of leaving for their own vacation, when they heard some frantic barking down below the pasture at the fish-pond. The pond had enough ice surface that would allow an unsuspecting dog to walk across it on the snow, but as it went further out towards the center, the ice would no longer support the weight of a 65-pound adventurous puppy! When Larry realized what had happened, they all ran down to the edge of the icy water. They immediately launched a small boat from the other side of the pond, and paddled hastily towards the nearly exhausted puppy, which was grasping futilely at the ever-cracking ice. He just could not get enough traction to pull his cold, water soaked body onto the solid surface, and he was tiring quickly. It would have been different had he been a polar bear.

Larry had arrived just in time, and it was then that we realized what the consequences would have been if he and his family had left their home 15 minutes earlier. We would never have known what happened to our buddy, as it is unlikely that we would have any clues as to how he died. The Good Lord was certainly watching over that boy! We rubbed him down with a large towel and he collapsed in front of the warm fireplace, where he soon drifted into a sound sleep, perhaps even dreaming about penguins and why they thought that cold water was fun!

When we thought about his future as an AKC champion, some doubts arose when we discovered that this ego trip would involve many miles of driving, and too much time spent out of house and office. The next alternative was to consider breeding him with whichever brown-eyed gorgeous blond Retriever of female persuasion that might be found in our little town. As time passed Dr. Jim told me about a neighbor of mine that had just such a creature at his house. The owner Bob was a Rotary Club member where I belonged, so I contacted him in order to get permission for such a venture. He was very accommodating, and we agreed to overlook any dowry or prenuptial arrangements. This would be a marriage made in "Heaven."

When Goldie was in heat, Bob piled her into his station wagon, and brought her to my house, in order to see if they were compatible. Since this was the first (to my knowledge!) attempt at love making for my big Red Boy, neither of us had a clue as to how to proceed. Fortunately another neighbor, who was far worldlier than any of us, was able to help the somewhat frustrated virgins into the position that might accomplish the purpose. After the pair were locked (is that the term?) he rearranged the position so that they were tail to tail? I wondered if he really knew what he or they were doing? We left them alone in the garage for a while, and when we returned they were separated and smoking a cigarette? (Just kidding!)

Goldie responded with a wink, and a wag of her tail as Bob came to take her home. Tawny Too was somewhat exhausted, and was happy to be left alone on his dog bed, probably reliving this experience with great pride and wonder.

After a few months, Bob called to tell me that the kids had to get married, because his baby Goldie was "with puppies". We were very excited, and agreed with Bob that we would like to have a female puppy as payment of the stud fee, and thought seriously that this could be a very productive way to enjoy dog ownership. There was also a valuable lesson in sex education that could be imparted to our curious children. Certain elements of the procedure would be deleted so as not to pique too much interest.

Missy & Tonsils
1978

CHAPTER 6

Enter Miss Missy

Our new puppy named "Missy" was a somewhat lighter shade of golden-red, and stayed with her mother and eight brothers and sisters for seven weeks or so. When we first went to bring the mother some flowers and dog treats, it was hard to peer at the nine adorable puppies, and only ask for one! However, the deal was for only one puppy, and we were more than satisfied. When the new arrival showed up Tawny Too gave her the once over and proceeded about his business. It was after all, only a little puppy, and he thought "who would pay any attention to her when I am around?"

Within six months we were to be further tested, as Tawny Too found that his hormones and keen sense of smell were meant to lead him into an adventure that he did not really want. Because of the fact that we wanted him to be able to meet other gorgeous girls, and perhaps exercise his newfound ability to add to the Golden world population, we left him untethered. When he was not in the fairly expansive yard that surrounded the house at dinnertime, we thought that he would be home before dark. He usually did not wander far after his last adventure at the lake.

He was not around in the early-morning either, and we began to explore some reasons for his being "AWOL." I called the local police chief, and alerted him about the disappearing act that had taken place. Then I called my friend Dr. Jim, to ask him for advice. He explained to me that young virile male dogs often do "overnight excursions," and that they usually make a bedraggled appearance at home within two days. He said that he would ask around the area since his practice covered most of the people in town, and someone would probably report the sighting of a new dog in the neighborhood. This was one of many varied advantages to living in a small town. A really big and better example would benefit us greatly in the future.

On the third day after his acute sensory apparatus led him off on a trail of some dog in heat, Dr. Jim received a phone call, that a large reddish Golden newcomer to the area had been sighted on Peterkin Hill, which is in South Woodstock. This was an area that was only two miles away as the crow flies, but 4 miles if you were not a crow, and needed a road to Jeep on. I happened to be home when he relayed this encouraging news to me, so I dashed off in the general direction of the location that was mentioned. We had no GPS in those days to make our search simpler, so we just had to search and seek the usual way. After about 45 minutes of winding around on little one lane gravel roads, which were the norm in the state of Vermont in the 60s, and are still fairly prevalent in 2008, I drove and stopped intermittently, to yell out his name every 3-400 yards in the area that had been where he was sighted. I saw no one in the area, but as my eyes focused on an old typical Vermont barn with unpainted, weathered boards, which were surrounded by a few nonfunctional farm implements, I got a glimpse of a moving creature. With two more loud calls, the object started to move towards me, and in a few seconds my exhausted Golden buddy bounded into my arms. He of course had a matted coat with some burrs attached, but he looked great to me as he gave me a loving doggy kiss. This would be no time to scold him, because he wouldn't know why I was upset. All he did was try to have a little fun and even meet a potential conquest. Maybe it was time to have this "Dude" neutered!

Missy, who really did not know what all the fuss was about, was happy to see her father and ran and jumped about, as she could see how happy the family was to have him back home. She did however, really enjoy the extra attention that she was the recipient of for the last two days. Everything went well for the next 18 months, as Missy grew into a very loving and quiet companion for her dad, and he seemed to settle down himself. We always felt that if you could afford the time and extra cost to have 2 dogs living under the same roof, it was beneficial to all concerned. In that way Goldens, in particular, who crave attention most of the time, can get it from their canine pal when you are not available.

A year later when Gwen and I were taking a short vacation to the Virgin Islands, we left the children and four legged friends in the hands of the babysitting husband and wife, Bobbi and Dick Roy, who were some of our nice young patients and friends. All went well, and after we returned home, we received a phone call from the local police chief who was fortunately a patient, and he told us that in our absence, Tawny Too and a next-door neighbor beagle dog had been caught chasing deer on a neighboring hill. In Vermont, dogs that chased deer were sometimes shot, because the dogs run across the frozen snow crust, while the sharp hoofed deer penetrate the crust and cannot move as quickly as normal. I was certain that Tawny Too would not participate in such an activity as killing, or even chasing a deer however the Police were certain of it, so now I was faced with a difficult decision. It is not fair to keep an active big dog chained up or made into a house pet, and so we had a family conference.

Our decision was to give Tawny Too, who had such good breeding, to a Golden Retriever kennel that could use him as a stud, and provide him with a good environment. We were very sad to leave him this way, however we did not want to have him shot, even though I was convinced that he would not attack a deer for any reason. He thought it to be fun, and had no malicious intent, as Goldens just don't do that!

So now we were down to our baby Missy, who was now two years old, but seemed content to provide us with a love that only a dog can provide. At least we thought that we were feeding only one dog, however she suddenly began to gain weight, and it didn't take a rocket scientist to figure out that she was pregnant. Tawny Too had arranged to leave behind the legacy of what turned out to be eight "Love children." This soon became chapter two in the sex education of children as she progressed toward motherhood. "Ain't love grand?"

Fortunately, we had enough backyard territory to handle the new family, and of course, we had four puppy sitters to take care of them. I really never appreciated how much fun was in store for us, as we followed the development of a new family. The gestation period was 60-64 days, and each day brought an obstetrical observance by the children, and some guesses as to when they would arrive, and how many will there be? The oft asked question of "Dad, can we each have one??" had to be carefully handled, and the final decision was "no!" We would keep the puppy that most resembled the father in color, and mother in gender.

62 days later, Gwen placed a call to my office that had a tone of panic in it, that requested the immediate presence of Dr. Butz at his residence. Do not stop at go, and try to be home in two minutes. As I quickly left a patient with a full mouth of cotton, my wide-eyed assistant prepared to play dentist for a few minutes. I mean "first things first, don't you know!"

When I arrived in the driveway, I was greeted by my wife, who steered me to the mudroom where Missy lay panting, and in some distress. I picked her up (no small task!) and placed her into the back of our station wagon, and we drove to a

Veterinarian that I did not know since Dr. Jim was not set up to do Caesarian section deliveries, and my office didn't want to try it either. The Clinic was only ten miles away, and Missy seemed to be holding up very well, so we were sure that we would be able to get her there on time. The clinic staff brought out a small stretcher device, and we were able to pile her on to it, and they whisked her away. A few minutes later, the veterinarian came through the door and told us that everything was fine, but that Missy would not deliver for a few hours, so we might as well go home, and call back later. This was fine with me, as my patient surely by now was getting tired of having her mouth full of cotton rolls.

Two days later, we drove to the animal hospital to pick up our new family. When we arrived back to our prepared nursery, we marveled at the miracle of birth whether canine or human, and how well this novice mother of eight was dealing with this situation. It was too early for us to even think about which of these tiny Golden treasures that we would claim and keep. Since many newborn puppies are not able to see, they keep themselves near to their mother, in a compact furry group, as they each tried to keep their little tummies full. Missy seemed as though she would wear her tongue out, as she continued to give each newborn the kind of "licking" far removed from the kind that children sometimes are exposed to. I often wondered how Tawny Too would have reacted to the results of his efforts if he were back in their presence. I am sure that he would have been a proud Papa, and enjoy the occasion as much as we all did.

Over the next two months we had to be practical about the matter, so we grudgingly sent out a newspaper ad to advertise the sale of seven "beautiful Golden Retriever puppies," while secretly hoping that no one would ever answer the ad. We knew that there was no way that we could keep them all, but how do you break up such a beautiful family? It didn't take long for us to have all of the puppies happily located in our area. It was fun to realize that this was the first dog that we ever had that was able to more than pay for her keep with her own personal income. Not enough however, to give any consideration towards opening up a kennel of our own. Missy slowly, but surely, regained her pre-puppy figure as she started up her new single parent life, with her beautiful, yet to be named, little girl puppy. It took a little while to make the transition from having only male dogs around to now have 2 beautiful affectionate females that again exhibited that "Velcro" characteristic that most Goldens have in their genes! The phrase "bonding" is one that is sometimes overused, however these two beautiful animals were almost always in constant contact whether snoozing on the sunlit porch, or chasing each other in the large backyard.

CHAPTER 7

Tonsils Is A Puppy??

We could not start out a new puppy's life with a moniker like "Runt," even though she was actually the smallest of the litter. A dog that was called anything that demeaning, would probably be so depressed that we would have to add Prozac to her kibbles before she was two years old. Our middle son, Brad was about to have his tonsils and adenoids removed, and of course was not overjoyed at the prospect of a trip to the hospital. Even promises of unlimited ice cream, and cold soda made him no less ready for the ordeal. I didn't explain to him that "in my day" patient's tonsils were removed in your home with the aid of a little bit of ether applied over the nostrils, using a large wad of cotton. Maybe that is where a lot of the ignorant "crackheads" got the idea that being a little high was really not a bad idea. Of course those folks are more likely to have a lobotomy in their future than a tonsillectomy.

Since "furball" had not received a real name that she would answer to, we decided to call her "Tonsils" as a tribute to Brad and his heroism. He was overjoyed at this prospect, and the puppy, newly christened, wagged her cute little tail. As Tonsils developed a beautiful shiny red gold lustrous coat that was passed by genes from her pop, she drew many an admiring glance from passerby's. She was however, the smallest of the Goldens that we had seen or owned, and probably never weighed more than 50 pounds. There was a huge Golden that belonged to a friend of mine in town that was called "Apollo," and he weighed 125 pounds. He looked almost like a St. Bernard, but did not have a small keg attached to his collar, therefore we all deemed him to be a real, very large Golden Retriever.

Missy and Tonsils were inseparable, and seemed to be always in contact even when they were asleep on the floor. Maybe this "touching thing" is found with all animals, but my experience with these two, and later versions, exhibited this behavior over and over. As an amateur photographer, it seems that most of my pictures that contain more than one animal show them in close contact with each other. Now that Missy had produced one litter of " Golden Goodies", it was felt that it would be expedient to ask Dr. Jim to intervene, and spay both of my beautiful little girls. After this procedure, we were able to relax and not worry about any more unexpected "puppy showers." We did not even have to construct a huge "invisible fence" on the property since they were both real "Home bodies."

With four children and seven acres of woodland, it was very easy to keep the two dogs occupied, and the exercise thereby derived made it easy for the entire gang to sleep through the night, all of the time. Since we did have enough acreage around the house, it was felt by popular demand, that there was a great need for a place for the water resistant coats of the four-legged critters, to be tested. It may have been my imagination, but I believe four of the yea votes were recorded by the small group known as "my heirs." So it was unanimous that a swimming pool was approved, and the necessary planning was undertaken. We lived on the outskirts of town, and the swimming pool was also needed as fire protection, since the nearest fire hydrant was one half a mile down the hill, and would not be of any assistance in a fire. It might even be a reason to have our insurance bill lowered. Having a pool was not only a wonderful advantage for the children, but was a significant help to us when we later experienced a fire.

Soon, the backhoe had a hole large enough for a 20 foot by 40 foot, plastic lined pool that would contain 26,000 gallons of clear, clean water delivered by milk trucks. As it turned out later, this water helped to partially save the house.

My next project was to design and construct a three small room bathhouse that also housed the filter system, and the propane heater. I enjoyed some help from the "zoo crew," in maintaining and cleaning the pool, but most of the time was spent by the dogs and children in the pool rather than out. I can't remember which group perfected the "Doggy paddle" first, but I did notice that the four nymphs were enjoying the diving board more than the puppies did. Dogs prefer to use the shallow end and stairway, much as senior citizens and small babies do. I have however, seen canines dive into the deep end, but they do not do well with the diving board.

Another friend, (we had a lot of friends in Vermont while building the swimming pool!), helped me do the cement work around the pool which was capped off with a nice 40 foot brick retaining wall, and four large slate steps, that went up to the deck and house. It is amazing how much money can be saved if you are able to perform these tasks yourself. It was hard work, but worth every minute. My main concern was to keep all of the digits on my hands, and more than once I came close to having to change my profession to something like a lawyer, but with the Lords' help, most of my wounds were not life threatening.

One of the things that was fun to watch was when one of the two dogs would run around the pool in hot pursuit of a wayward frog. I can't imagine the terror that the frogs experienced, when they looked up and saw those giant jaws only a foot away. When they thought that it was trapped in a corner, they reached down to find that it had submerged and escaped. We tried to keep the dogs out of the pool most of the time, since their fine hair caused problems with the filtration system. But what did they care?

As the years went on John and Deb, our oldest 2 children would make a little school money, by giving swimming lessons to local children. They, along with my wife, provided swimming experiences to a group of village children that had handicaps, some quite severe, and I am not sure who had the most fun, but all benefited from those lessons. Another example of what wonderful benefits are derived from small town living. We would soon find out just how much of those benefits would be returned to us, in so many ways.

During the summer of 1973, our nearby ski area to the west was inundated with a steady rainstorm that lasted for three days. When you live in Vermont, there are many mountains that provide skiing pleasure in the winter, hiking in this summer, as well as spectacular scenery all year long. The fall foliage is known around the world, and the beautiful spring vistas are also glorious. These mountains also provide a watershed of vast proportions, so that even though you may live many miles from the mountain peaks, you will feel the effects of a major rainstorm almost at any altitude. The town of Woodstock is about 30 miles from the ski areas of Killington Mountain with a small river called the "Ottauquechee," an Indian word meaning "smiling waters," running down and through the center of town. Normally the water is barely deep enough to run a rubber raft all the way down through, but during this July, the river was going to rise 22 feet in just 2 days. This obviously would create many problems with the homes and businesses that line the river from the mountain top 40 miles west to the juncture of this river and the confluence with the White River and later the Connecticut River. Fortunately, there is a flood control dam, which served its purpose well, but the damage was done before the dam was reached. The water reached a height of over 100 feet at the base of the dam. The water that was held back by this amazing engineering feat would have done tremendous damage to the town of White River Jct, and other towns south of it. The river would then flow into the White River and on to the Connecticut River, ending in the Atlantic Ocean eventually.

My oldest son John, and I went down into the town to see the damage, but really had no idea how far reaching this flood was to be. As we watched from the beautiful wooden covered bridge, that separates two parts of the village, we would see a sight that seemed unbelievable at the time. About a mile upstream there was a Gas and Electric company that was set upon the banks of the river. Its large storage area contained empty propane tanks of all sizes. Some tanks were 1000-gallon tanks, and all were being floated away, to cruise down the river like a flotilla of white submarines. Some that had been connected were hissing as they passed by, as the remaining gas was expelled. My son was later to get a job with this company to track down the flying gas tanks when they ceased running down the river. This work continued for many weeks after the flood subsided. As we watched this powerful wave of water taking everything in its path, we realized what a major problem that this posed. When I went to the house of one of my patients to help him move his furniture from the basement, to the second floor, in order not to lose it, John drove back to the house to get his camera so that he could record this historical event. He was gone for five hours, taking photos all up and down the river, which he later made into a small book about the "Flood of 73." This would be remembered as the second largest flood of the century in our area.

After feeling blessed that we had not received any damage from the flood, life got back into its normal semi-hectic mode, and we celebrated the Christmas holiday with all of the children at home. Christmas always seems to be a little extra nice when you have brisk cold, clear days that involve sledding, skiing, or ice skating, all of which are found in Vermont for a period of at least three months. Missy and Tonsils both received their Christmas stockings with all sorts of glorious squeeze toys, and chicken flavored treats. Every chance she got, Tonsils would take a piece of the wrapping paper that someone has meticulously prepared, and render it into a pile of shredded pieces. The puppies had no clue about the real meaning of this family gathering, but they were going to take advantage of this opportunity to receive some loving caresses from all of us. They didn't have that large a group of people around that many times of the year. I don't think that any animal seeks, receives, and longs for affection as much as a Golden Retriever. They thrive on it and they know that we like it too. Sometimes these dogs have boundless energy, and will retrieve until their tongues nearly reached the ground, but will at a moments notice lay down next to you, and give you a loving lick on what ever part of you that they can reach. Heaven help you if you have recently perspired, because the salt from your body is irresistible. They have so many of the good qualities of mankind in their repertoire that one sometimes wishes that there were more Goldens in the Universe than humans. So much for wishful thinking!

After enjoying the real meaning of Christmas at our local Congregational Church, the family spent the next few days playing recreational games, and making sure that we would all need to go on some type of diet program in order to reach New Year's eve, and have any clothes that still fit. This reprieve from school was soon over, and the children were about to get back to their books, and the year was celebrated on New Year's Eve. It was a wonderful period of family love and appreciation, celebrated with our four children and 2 pups. No one had any idea what 1974 would bring, and unfortunately, it would unfold as a year no one of us would want to see again!

CHAPTER 8

The Hoof and Mouth Trophy

I had already gotten the reputation of being one who never allowed the patient to answer a single question that was put to them. The patients never understood that my verbal diarrhea was a ploy to fool them into a state of mind, that mentally at least, let them relax their semi-rigid bodies, so that I could work with them. The dentist loses no time or money if he talks nonstop, but does lose both, if he allows the patient to ever get out an answer. We at least try to ask questions that really do not require a sensible answer. Questions such as, "Did that hurt a little?" or "Are you ready to have your root canal now?" do not really need an answer, nor did we want to hear one. Dentistry today is vastly different than when I started in 1950s, but we tried to make it as painless as possible and usually succeeded.

Dr. Jim and I played golf usually after Rotary Club meeting every Wednesday afternoon rain or shine, and neither of us ever worked a Wednesday afternoon in the summer. We replaced golf with paddle tennis in the wintertime, with the same golfing group, which consisted of between 8 to 12 other avid sportsmen.

One of our golfing group had been a very fine athlete who was the recipient of many varied awards, plaques and trophies. He found one that was made of silver, and resembled the Ryder Cup trophy, only smaller. He presented it to Jim and I to be recognized as the official "Hoof and Mouth Trophy." Jim promptly went out to a trophy store and ordered five three-inch round medals on a 20 inch chain, that showed a golfer on the front and inscribed on the back was "Hoof and Mouth Winner 1975". Similar medals were made up for the next four years. The winner of the last game of the calendar year was to keep the trophy for the year, and retain the medal permanently. The loser would be responsible for a cocktail party-dinner for the 12 or so other participants that played with us during the year.

One particular year was memorable, because I had won the last match in Vermont, in November, and was in Florida in December. In order to meet the requirement of calendar year, Jim called, and said that he and his wife Dot were coming down to Florida the week before New year's, and that I must be prepared to defend the title one more time this year. He really did not want to give up this valued trophy. It happened that one of my son's was there in Florida for the holidays, and unbeknownst to us was video taping the event covertly, so that there would not be any chance of guessing who that years' winner really was. As luck would have it, I beat him again with proof, and he and

Dot returned sadly to Vermont to face another winter without the trophy.

One of the trophy presentation parties was held at Dr. Jims' house in December, because he had lost again. He asked Gwen and I if we could come to this gala in some sort of formal attire, because of the importance of this event. This was not common dress in rural Vermont, but I put on a tuxedo and Gwen dressed as a gorgeous flapper from the roaring 20s. As we approached Jim's house and office combination, we saw a few cars, so I knew that the party was on. However, it was very quiet, and not what you expect from this group after a few drinks. As I opened the outside door, I noticed a black satin ribbon draped across the entrance. We started towards the kitchen, and a black cat appeared with another black satin ribbon around its neck. There was only ominous silence as we moved toward the dining room. There was certainly something strange going on. At the entrance door of the dining room stood Dr. Jim in a black suit to greet us, and we began to hear the sound of a funeral dirge in the background. "This is really weird!" we both thought, and then peered into the room at a large table set with a black tablecloth, and in the center of the table was a white satin box, in which lay the "Hoof and Mouth "Trophy," on its' side as if in a casket. What a picture! Behind the table was another figure dressed in black with a black beard and a top hat that Lincoln would have loved. The rest of the room was silent, as we looked past the casket and saw three small rows of folding chairs, again adorned with black ribbon.

The chairs were occupied by our golfing group and spouses, all in mourning clothes with bowed heads, some even had black ash marks on their foreheads. It was a very touching moment, and everyone was taking it very seriously, for the moment! The music was furnished by our local undertaker, and was quite appropriate. It was the funniest thing we had ever seen, and to top it off, there was a bar set up behind the mourners, and all of the liquor bottles had the," you guessed it "black satin" bows attached to each neck. Then everybody got up and started to laugh until near crying. It was marvelous, especially the music and the demeanor of the group. Once I recovered my sensibilities, I called back to my home, where sons John, Brad and Jim were home for the holidays, and summoned them to rush right over (about three miles), and bring a camera because I did not want to ever forget this picture. No one of course would ever attempt to outdo this celebration, and never could. It was perfect and this tournament lasted until Jim died in 1997.

CHAPTER 9

The Fire of '74

On January 18th, 1974, an event that would be the biggest change in our lives unexpectedly occurred. It was a typically frigid day with temperatures reaching minus 5 degrees when I arrived home for dinner from the office. It was pleasant since the memories of the Christmas holiday were still fresh, and some decorations were still scattered throughout the house. The house was filled with the odor of the soon to be served dinner. Then as Gwen gave me a greeting kiss, she calmly told me that she had had difficulty getting our relatively new station wagon started today, because it was so cold. I turned and went directly to the garage that I had just parked my Jeep in, next to my garden tractor that now served as a snow blower. My Jeep was also equipped with a plow, and I loved to show my skill at mass snow removal whenever the occasion arose which was often in Vermont. After a few tries I was able to get the wagon started, and I laid a brick on the accelerator pedal, in order to keep the engine running at a speed that would soon recharge the frigid battery. This was an operation that I had performed a multitude of times on cold days. I noticed the smell of gasoline however, but that was normal when a car has been flooded in the starting process. With task completed I returned to the house through a breezeway that connected the garage to the house, and left the car purring in the garage.

The dining room was a large room that was an extension of the kitchen and contained a beautiful antique cherry expansion table that could expand to accommodate up to 12-14 guests. As fate would have it, this room had one wall that was designed as a mini-library, and was filled from top to bottom with all manner of books, most of them were old, and represented the entire collection of my grandfathers medical books, and complete sets of famous American authors. I think that my grandfather was an easy mark for some salesman, because very few of these books had ever been actually read, or even moved for fifty years. They looked a little bit like the mountain of matching sets of books that you see in any lawyers' office. Maybe they looked at theirs, but I don't think so. It was probably more important that their covers blended in with the decorators theme than whether or not they were of any academic value. I was in the process of decorating our new office at the local Health Center, and I had removed many of the framed photographs and paintings that had been collected over the years, that were hanging in the house. I was going to take them to the office to see which ones could work well on the bare walls, and I had lined them up together

---

on the dining table. There were at least 20-25 pieces of art, and some of them were one of a kind, that were not listed as National Treasures, but did have considerable emotional appeal and value to us since many were painted by patients and friends.

Because the dining room now resembled a cluttered gallery, it was necessary for us to dine in the basement playroom that I had built a few years earlier. The children were all gone at the time, as some were visiting local friends, and some away at school. At approximately 8:00 p.m., the room suddenly became pitch dark, and it was evident that we had lost our electricity, but why? In the winter, it is not unusual for ice storms to create short circuits in the electrical transformers that are high on the poles, resulting in blackouts. However this was different, as I soon found out, and when I moved to look out of our small basement window, and observed that the entire area was lit up with orange and red shades of color that were very ominous. I said to Gwen "this is not a transformer problem!" as we raced up the steps to the kitchen and rushed to the back door. Missy and Tonsils were right on our heels as we went through the unlighted kitchen. At that moment at least, we were not able to smell any of the telltale smoke aromas that are associated with fire, however I am sure that both dogs had detected the unusual odor long before we were aware, but they had no way of knowing what was happening.

We were aghast, as the shock of seeing the garage in flames nearly overpowered us, and we had no electricity, since the wires that went through the garage had already burned. This meant that there was no phone, so we were unable to report the fire. This was terribly frustrating however, the fire had already been reported to the Fire Dept. by some folks who were sleighing on Mount Tom, which was directly across the small valley from our hillside location. Gwen and I started out of the house to call a neighbor, and phone the firehouse. I stopped in front of the garage, and wanted to quickly get into my Jeep, which might be saved from its burning garage mate. Gwen however, grabbed me and said, "I love you and you are not going in there!" Discretion taking over, I decided she was right so we raced down the driveway, and within seconds a fiery explosion took what was left of the station wagon and engulfed the little Jeep, along with my beautiful International Harvester tractor in flames. It had plowed its last road! She was right again, and I was thankful for her good sense. What are wives for, eh?? I can always buy another 4 wheeler!

Gwen and I ran down the street towards the next house on the road with the 2 dogs trailing behind, not knowing what was going on. When we reached our nearest neighbor, 500 yards away, we found no one home, and proceeded down the road to the next house. As we ran hard we could hear the snapping and crackling noises that only are heard coming from a fire, the fire that was consuming our property. There was nothing to do but continue on with the dogs, which would not leave us under any circumstances. I did not want to look at the conflagration on the hill to my right, and I didn't learn until later, why I could not hear any shrieking sirens making their way rapidly to the fire. Where were they??

I wondered if I should have stayed at the house while Gwen went on to the other house, in order to save as much as I could since the fire had not actually reached the main structure yet. It is easy to say, after the fact, that there was only material stuff in the house, and you should not take any chances with your life, however, it always crosses your mind that many things could have been removed from the house before the fire went any further. I am sure that many foolish folks have lost their lives making the wrong decision, but it was certainly tempting to be a macho man!

We made it to the next house, still in sight and sound of our burning house, and knocked on the door of our 85-year-old neighbor, grandmotherly, old Alice Kilner who was still as mentally capable as anyone her age, and could tell that something was terribly wrong. After we explained the situation, we sat in her living room, as Gwen began to cry when she started to realize what this really meant. That was the home that we built together, and now it was going to be gone. One of the ironies of this situation was that after 14 years of occupancy, we had just completed the whole interior of the dwelling, including the wallpapering of the plaster walls that I had steadfastly refused to cover with anything but paint. As it turned out the plaster surfaces made it much easier to redo, as sheetrock would have all been replaced. The inside had also been repainted, and our broken-hearted contractor had not even sent us a bill for services. When he arrived at the house a few days after the fire, he had tears in his eyes after all of the hard work he and his men had performed, that now was all destroyed. He could not have been more discouraged if it had been his own home. There was absolutely nothing that did not have to be completely redone.

After Alice had settled us down, and I drank the glass of Scotch that she graciously provided me with, we finally heard the fire trucks, and the unbelievable volunteer fire department descending on the blazing structure. I still did not want to go back up on the hill to the house, until the fire chief, a longtime patient and friend, came to Alice's door, to see if I wanted to visit the house now that the fire was in control, so as to assess the damage. It was devastating to see the interior of the building with smoke stained walls and water dripping from the ceilings. Everything inside the two-story house with basement was either soot covered or unrepairable, with few exceptions. The major items that might be restored were our cherry grand piano, and a basement pool table, which was also an antique. It had a chance to go another 100 years, and is still in service today at one of my son's home. The garage and its contents of motor vehicles and tools was completely gone, with only the burnt bodies of the cars standing amongst piles of unrecognizable objects that once had a meaning and purpose.

The beautiful redwood deck that I had built was now charcoal, with only a few 2 by 4's left, that I later built into a picnic table that still sits in the yard of our present home as a reminder that never is everything lost. The west end of the house that was attached to the garage by a breezeway was mostly destroyed, but the main structure was 75 percent structurally unaffected. The major job was to clean up the smoke and sooty walls, and to try to eliminate the pervasive smell of burning materials. This is a monumental chore that required many helpful hands and a ton of magic cleaners. All of the windows were broken in order to let out the gases and heat that were created inside the house.

Gwen's beloved kitchen was a complete shambles, and nothing in it was retrieved. A fireman was kind enough to remove the multitude of houseplants that were her favorites, and placed them in neat rows outside the house. However, it was a labor of love wasted, as the freezing temperatures outside would not allow any live plant to survive, and they didn't, but the thought was there. I walked around the house with the Chief, and he asked me if there was anything that I would like to remove from the structure? I went into the den and retrieved my camera bag that contained film and various lenses, as I knew that I would have to photograph the destruction for insurance purposes. I was happy to learn later, that all of our family photos were safe in the basement, and suffered no damage. After a quick perusal of the entire house, I determined that I might as well go back to Alice's house, where she did her best to console Gwen. My wife did not want to have to look at the mess that once was her pride and joy, but would be again, if I had anything to do about it. There was no doubt in my mind that we would rebuild the house and make some changes that would actually be better than before. The first one would be to move the new garage 50 feet from the main house. Smart, eh? The firemen would stay for many hours more, checking for hot spots that might flare up again, and it was around midnight when they returned to the station. Their job was well done, but ours was just beginning, and it would be a difficult one.

Now that the shock was over, I started on the long trip back to normalcy, by picking up the phone, and calling my friend and patient, Max Boynton whose strong back and hands had helped me plan and construct the house originally. Building a home in Vermont is different than any moderate temperature area, and special techniques had to be applied. The most important of which had to do with the mainframe and roof, which had to be built to withstand very heavy loads of snow and ice, that sometimes were 36 inches deep. The fact that the house was so well crafted made it easier to rebuild, and that was what we all did, and it took six months to finish the job. I spent as much time as I could to help his men, and they often worked on Sundays to speed up the process.

One of the other reasons that we could start rebuilding right away was that the heating system of the house was intact except for the zone where the flames had invaded. The windows were all covered with plywood sheets and the oil-fired system was turned up to the maximum temperature, so as to dry the house up, while the fire-ravaged end of the house was covered with huge, blue polyethylene sheets. Everything inside the house was saturated with the water that was necessary to fight the fire, but luckily I had placed two floor drains in the finished basement when I designed it, and they performed very well, as they allowed the water to drain out from the house to the outside.

Earlier, I mentioned that our swimming pool was a lifesaver, and the Lord must have given me the insight to build it. We had no access to fire hydrants since we were above the level that water pressure could reach. Fire fighters had to trust that their tanker trucks would provide enough water to handle a fire, and we had no pond on the property. This didn't work for us, but the alert firemen knew that I had a swimming pool in the backyard. There is that "small town" idea proving itself a valuable asset again! They found the pool covered with snow and ice, and had to break through 2 inches of ice to get at the 26,000 gallons of house saving water. Without this ability to have an extra supply of water we all were sure that the structure would have been leveled to the ground.

It was not until the next day, that I was able to find out why the response to the fire was delayed for forty minutes, a major factor in the amount of damage that resulted. In the decade of the 70s, there were no such niceties as the electronic gadgets that in today's world adorn the belt of every man, woman, child and fire fighter. All we had was a regular telephone that was not able to reach the majority of the fire fighters, many of whom were attending a pre-marital party at a local meeting house. Once they arrived at the scene, they did a marvelous job, and I found no fault with them or their actions. It was just one of those unfortunate occurrences that sometimes complicate our lives. But I later lobbied in town meetings for a better and more comprehensive Police and Fire rapid response system.

For some unknown reason, there were two more house fires in town that same year, and two teenagers set fire to, and extensively damaged, the beautiful wooden covered bridge in the center of the Historical area of Woodstock. I can't understand why some ignorant people just can't be happy, unless they are destroying someone else's property! It is bad enough when accidents happen but willful acts of senseless destruction serve no purpose.

In the morning after the fire, Gwen and I gathered ourselves, with the dogs, and walked up to the house site. Our hearts sunk as we looked at the devastation that had taken place only hours earlier. Missy and Tonsils started immediately to search and sniff out the entire area around the charred section of the house that had been their sleeping room. They even were able to find their metal food and water dishes that had been able to survive the heat and flames. I had a camera, and started to photograph every room in the house from different perspectives, as I knew this was necessary for the insurance claim to follow. For anyone who has not experienced a fire first hand, the aroma that remains after the fact is one that you will not want to relive. The smoke that permeates every nook and cranny of the house also leaves a permanent reminder of what took place. In the furthest bedroom from the actual active burning area, there was a bureau drawer of clothes that belonged to one of the boys. As each item of clothing was removed from the drawer, you could see the distinct outline of each item on the bottom of the drawer itself, etched by the smoke.

All of the clothing, draperies, bed linens, and mattresses were ruined, even though not actually burned. Some wooden items were able to be refinished, and we did keep a local antique dealer quite busy for a long period, redoing them to their natural original condition. In some incidences they looked better than they did before, which again proved the old saying "Out of all bad comes some good." I even got a new set of golf clubs, while the puppies would get to enjoy the comfortable new beds that they received.

Within a few hours after we arrived at the house, all manner of people started to fill our driveway. Most were our amazing "small town" friends, and some just wanted to see for themselves what actually happened. At least we knew that there would not be any looters or thieves, because in those days most Vermonters usually didn't even lock their houses or cars when they were away. This is somewhat true even today, but I wouldn't count on it.

Two friends greeted us as we shared the coffee, juice and pastries that were donated by our friend Bob Barton, the manager of the Rockresort, Woodstock Inn. They wanted us to know that there were two completely furnished houses in the Village that we could move into immediately, dogs and kids included. Our local Ford dealer, Mait Blake also saw to it that we had a station wagon to use for an unlimited time at no charge. No doghouses were offered, so the pups had to stay at our newly rented home in the village with us. Many folks brought us clothing to wear, and large quantities of food began to arrive at the rental house immediately. We could have fed an Army! The sun was beginning to break through the dark clouds that had been cast over our lives, and we were so happy to belong to such a loving community! I would be able to return to work immediately, and that was even more important at this stage of our lives.

At the time of the fire, I was the chairman of the local school board and a Deacon of our Congregational church, which helped account for the scores of bodies that began to organize from the teachers and church organizations that began to step in to clean up the mess that once was Pine View One. The local supermarket even donated boxes of detergents, bleach, and all types of cleaning tools, which included mops, brooms and scouring pads. In a matter of weeks, the house had every bit of debris removed, and the walls, ceilings and floors had been scraped and scrubbed, leaving us in an almost livable condition. More was needed, but the initial surge was the hardest and most important. Everyone was so helpful and nice, and demonstrated how real Americans respond to tragedy and need. Gwen and I knew, as did the children, what a truly wonderful town that we lived in and would continue to live in.

It was not until the day after the fire that we got the news that one of the fire fighters had managed to retrieve the cat that our daughter had brought home as a trial to see if our puppies or us, for that matter, could tolerate another critter. I have to admit that the only cats that I really love are Siberian tigers, and they are not easily kept in a home environment. Those powerful, graceful, creatures with the big glorious blue eyes that you would love to hug, if you only were sure that you would survive. At any rate, our daughter Debby had talked us into giving the cat a chance to charm us. This poor kitty didn't even get to try out her nine lives, as she did not survive the first night at Dr. Jim's hospital. She died of smoke inhalation, as she tried to escape the fire by hiding out in the far reaches of the basement. It was very fortunate that Missy and Tonsils followed us out of the house in the beginning of the fire, because even though they possess great intelligence, it is doubtful that they could have survived on their own.

Many are the times that we thanked God for allowing us to escape this horrible event with only losing the life of the poor cat. No humans were injured, no dogs were hurt, and most of the loss was restricted to material possessions, which we all agreed was a great lesson learned, that has benefited the children in particular. "Things" can be replaced, but life is sacred and needs to be protected, and cannot be replaced. I believe that our children learned more about the values of life through this tragedy than they could have in any other way. Many of the objects in the house were one of a kind and would be missed, of course, but most of us have too much stuff anyway.

I sat down in the comfort of our new temporary home, that the puppies easily adapted to, and started to make drawings of the changes that I wanted to make in the renovation of what would now be called, Pineview II. The one thing that I vowed to change was the location of a new garage, which now would be at least fifty feet away from the main structure. This idea must have had "Divine guidance", because 15 years later when the house had new owners, the garage again was gutted by fire, this time caused by hot charcoal ashes that were placed into a trash container. This time however, there was no damage incurred by the main house. Fortunately, there were no automobiles in it either.

This must have been the "Chinese year of the fire," or something weird like that, because another car spontaneously caught fire in the village within 2 months. This time it was a Porsche, and no other damage resulted, however it was quite a coincidence. The second event that sent chills up our spine took place 4 months after we moved into the rental house, and involved the beautiful wooden covered bridge in town only 300 yards away from our rental home. We could actually see the flames from the burning bridge from our dining room window, and it was a frightening spectacle to say the least. We had not seen anything actually in flames for many years, and suddenly this was happening, what was going on?? It was getting very difficult to sleep at night without having a nightmare. This time it was an intentional torching of this important landmark.

This was an exact copy of the original bridge, and was constructed with no nails, bolts or any new hardware, as wooden pegs were used to secure the pieces. The main structure was actually drawn across the river by several large draught horses.

The two teenagers were caught, and since the bridge was only one half charred, it could be repaired. If I had ever been the judge that oversaw this case, I would have chained those two kids to the bridge, under permanent restraint, until they physically cleaned up all of the destruction that they imparted to the bridge. It is now still in use, and no one could ever tell by looking at it that it had ever gone through this man made ordeal!

After a period of quiet time, we resumed our practice and home activities, as we began to plan how to refurbish the new house. One day the mail delivered a letter from the insurance company, that contained a check for $25,000 dollars, as partial payment for our claim. At that moment, I had never seen such a large check, and my mind went a little askew as I contemplated what I could buy with that large sum of money. It was true that it would replace some objects, but insurance claims checks never are able to cover anywhere near the real expenditures that will have to be made to return the property to its original state. Another lesson learned by the entire family!!

Whenever any of the family had some spare time, we would go up to the property and work on scrubbing the blackened walls with a special scent-removing detergent, but it seemed like an endless task. There were times when we wondered if having a large home was a benefit, or a big disadvantage, since the walls seemed to go on forever. We were able to observe the progress that Max and his men were making, and that gave us a great deal of encouragement. Some of the changes that I had designed actually made the house better suited for the whole family than it was before. We ended up with a bigger mudroom for the dogs, and a larger family room with a fireplace, which helped to heat the house as well. You do live and learn, and we were really learning a lot!

As spring came a milk tanker truck arrived in the backyard, and made the first of several deliveries of water into the depleted swimming hole known formerly as the pool. I can still remember watching as the milk truck backed down the hill toward the pool to unload its supply of new water, and I wondered what would happen if the brakes did not work, and the truck ended up in the pool! It took 3 loads of water to get the level back to where it was before the fire. This pool had not only partially saved this house, but it incurred no damage itself.

Tonsil & Missy
1978

CHAPTER 10

Out of the Ashes

July arrived, and we were back in full force in the nearly all-new home at last. It was 6 months of real hard, but gratifying labor. Our spirits had been bolstered by the great favors that friends bestowed upon us. The children received the news that Bernard, a friend that was in the ski outfitting business, had purchased at his cost, beautiful new metal skis, poles and boots that would play a large part in the next winter activities. Needless to say in Vermont, skiing is really important and the kids loved it. As you may remember from an earlier chapter in the book, skiing was not one of my favorite activities, but I was pleased that the children were able to enjoy it along with their mother, who actually taught the activity to little kids who didn't know any better! Even with the advent of non-breakable metal skis, I went to the slopes as seldom as I could. They had yet to invent break proof bones, and I was not going to take any chances, despite weathering the challenges of bringing up 4 children.

One of the best favors was performed by good friends, Betty and Tom McGuire, who were interior decorators, and had helped us to furnish the house when we moved in originally. Boy, were we in need of a decorator! They told us that they would be able to replace all of the interior articles including drapes, carpets, and some furniture at their cost, and the savings to us would be tremendous. The car had been replaced with another station wagon, and my new garden tractor shared the newly located garage with it. There were a lot of nice replacement items, and at least that was one of the benefits received from the horrible event. Not that I ever wanted to experience another fire, but there was a certain amount of pleasure involved, when you could go out and replace nearly all of the items that you once thought to be important and necessary with brand new ones.

A few months later, when the children were back in school, we received a call from Debby, our daughter, who was attending the University of Vermont in Burlington. She had been playing "Broom Ball", a version of ice hockey that was played on ice, but with brooms instead of sticks, She had torn a ligament in her left knee, and would require an operation. The good news was that the hockey team's top surgeon was very competent in the repair of knees as it was a common injury in winter sports. He had agreed to perform the tricky surgery, and it was very successful. She then returned home to "Pineview II," and became the first recovering patient to rehabilitate in the newly refurbished house.

Even the new furniture in the house did not include a hospital bed, and we did not have an elevator, so it was decided that she could best be served as an occupant of the first floor living room in a sofa bed. It was in this homespun recovery room, that she was to audition our latest member of the Golden family. Except for the fact that she was in a complete leg cast, it was really a very nice place to recover from injuries as the sun shone brightly over the snow covered hills, and it was cozy and warm in front of a real brick fireplace. It was far better than any hospital room could have been, and the nursing staff was always on duty. Even Missy and Tonsils were able keep her company, but were not allowed to jump onto the makeshift bed, even though I am sure that they did have that in mind!

One day during her recovery time, a man who was on the board of our local Health Center, where my office was located, had been looking around my waiting area and seen some of my photographs of present and past dogs. Gwen happened to be working with me, as she frequently did, as a receptionist and part-time assistant. He gazed at the photos, and inquired of her, "Are these your dogs?" When she proudly answered in the affirmative, he asked her if the family would enjoy another retriever to add to their present collection. Since this was the first free Golden that we had never been offered, this gift merited some serious consideration. There had to be a catch, as no one would willingly dispose of a real Golden retriever.

He explained that his dog was four years old, and had hip dysplasia, which is quite common in Golden Retrievers, and he also lost too much hair to remain long in his wife's good graces. He mentioned. that even though the dog came from a decent kennel in Connecticut, that he had decided to have the dog "put down." Gwen tried her hardest to smile, and said "nobody should ever put a Golden down for those reasons, please bring him to our home and we will see how he gets along with our other two dogs."

True to his word, the next morning he brought the big dog to the house, and when he reached the kitchen, the dog made a beeline for the living room, that was Deb's private hospital room. I have no idea how he knew that anyone was there, as he had never been in this house! She lay on a sofa bed with her large plaster cast making comfort next to impossible, and when the dog saw her, he ran directly to the bed, and put his two large front paws onto the bed and attempted, in a clumsy way, to plant a doggy kiss on Deb's surprised face. As the big dog acted like a long lost friend, our decision was cast, and we told the gentleman "if you leave quietly now, we shall be very happy to take over care of your dog and thank you very much." What a wonderful surprise as this new addition came into our lives even though he was not as physically handsome as our previous dogs had been, and he did shed hair easily, we knew that everything would work out well.

His name was "Squire," and he worked very well into our home regimen. We were now beginning to look a bit like a kennel, but no one was complaining. Because of Squires' dysplastic condition, he was not able to keep up with the other dogs, in their jaunts around the yard, even though he was younger and larger than either Missy or Tonsils. Both of the females were now spayed, and Squire, in his gentlemanly way did not seem interested in anything sexual even though these two were "hot looking chicks," in the vernacular of today! This was an interesting contrast to the way that Tawny Two would have behaved. The girls were both happy and safe, and thoroughly enjoyed outrunning the partially crippled male, whenever it came to ball retrieval duties. He gave his best effort, but was in no way up to the task, and it must have been hard on his male ego to be constantly outshone by his adopted sisters. The only time that Squire showed his mastery over the girls was when they tried to sneak some of his dog food. He turned them quickly away with a low growl, and they understood that he was not in the mood to play games all of the time! However, we were all one big happy family!

All went well for a few years, and only changed when I came out one morning to the mud room, where the three dogs had their separate beds, and found Missy, lying motionless on her bed. As the other two dogs greeted me with their usual tail wagging and bright brown eyes, there was still no movement from this lovable creature, and it didn't take long for me to kneel by her side, and see that she had passed away, quietly and with no signs of stress or pain at any time. She had just drifted away, and was now with her mate, and so another chapter of "My 50 Golden Years" had been written, and she would not be forgotten. It was a beautiful finish to her life, and she had given us as much love as she possibly could, and had provided us with Tonsils as a bonus. She was only ten years old.

Tonsils now played in the yard with the same vim and vigor that she had exhibited with her mother, and since Squire was a bit slower, dragging his slightly crippled legs, she was always able to stay ahead of him, however he would always keep plugging away. Whenever they both arrived at a thrown ball at the same time, he was very adept at using his larger body to block her path enough to get to the ball first. She would then counter by quickly snatching the ball up when he took a moment to get his breath back, and run off with it again. He could only stand there and with a wistful look on his face, say to himself "I'll get you someday kid." Even though Squire was not an old dog, he generally behaved as if he was much older. His coat was a bit scraggly with strains of white hair mixed in with his lighter beige original fur covering. His squarish large head started to grey up around his muzzle almost like a canine version of a "Got Milk" commercial, and continued to change more each year. It was strange that he lived to be older than all of our other Goldens, even while appearing to age more than any of them. This proved the old saying about "Just because there is snow on the roof doesn't mean that the fire has gone out! "Even though his dysplastic hips kept him from racing about, there was never a time when he did not try to keep up with all of them even when he must have been suffering significant pain. You could tell by looking into his eyes that he wished that he could keep up with those young-uns, but it was never going to be possible!

One early fall day, before any hunting season began, we were driving up the road just in front of our property at a reasonable pace, because dozens of deer were constantly crossing the road to reach the area behind our house that was overgrown with wild apples. We were always careful driving in that particular area, because the deer had a terrible habit of appearing out of nowhere, at almost any moment, and paid little heed to a moving vehicle. It is almost as if they feel invulnerable, only we know differently. Suddenly, from the right side of the road, two large does bolted across our bow, barely missing our car, and with tails held high, bounded into the woods next to us. Then along came a smaller deer that was trailing its mother, and slammed into our right front fender, and dropped to the ground. Since we were almost at a standstill, I jumped out of the car and found myself close to the fallen young deer that turned out to be a button-horn buck. That is a very young male whose antlers are just forming. Our "Bambi like" friend was lying quietly on the asphalt, and I could quickly see that his left leg appeared to be broken, as well as his mandible (jaw).

I stroked his head, and could feel the fear that he was experiencing, and felt badly, but knew that we had no way of avoiding the collision. Since we were so close to home, I was able to reach a phone in our neighbor's house, which was only 30 yards away. We almost thought about calling Dr. Jim, to see if he could care for the deer, but instead I called the local police. The beautiful little guy laid quietly until the police car arrived, and as people approached him, panic took over and the deer tried to get up on his three good legs, and climb the steep embankment alongside the road. His efforts went for naught, as he kept slipping back down the slippery bank, and the policeman drew his pistol, and for what ever reason I do not know, took two shots to take the animal out of his misery.

The police checked my car for damage, and asked me if I would like the carcass. Being a normal hunting type, I answered, "of course I would," and spent a few minutes signing the necessary paperwork, and then handed it over with a $5.00 fee. Now the dead bundle of venison all wrapped in a beautiful brown fur coat was my responsibility. Since we love deer meat, I immediately took him to our garage, and then did the necessary work to field dress the lifeless deer. I had done this a few times before while hunting in the deep Maine woods, but never hunted around the house, since these were considered our pets. I called Dr. Jim and explained what had happened, and he agreed to come over immediately, and help me learn how to properly prepare the meat for human consumption. He would in effect be a highly trained butcher.

This unusual bit of activity in the garage aroused the interests of my two "Guard dogs" as they both got a scent of the dead stranger in the area They bounded towards us with their noses a quarter-inch above the ground, until they were only a few feet from the remains. I never could figure out how these dogs could run at top speed, and keep their noses to the ground, without getting a nose burn, this is similar to rug burn, the children get when wrestling in the living room.

As Dr. Jim and I played out the role of "Supermarket Meat Department," the small piles of venison chops, steaks, roast and meat to be used for ground meat, were lined up on our small wooden work table that I am sure looked to the bewildered dogs like a view of 'Puppy Heaven." Since the garage door was fully open, the furry critters kept sneaking closer to us as we toiled at our important task. Suddenly, in a lightning like move, Tonsils with the deft touch of an efficient shoplifter, grabbed a couple of the raw steaks in her teeth and bounded out of the garage with Squire following close behind. I dropped my meat cleaver and ran into the yard only 10 yards behind the little innocent looking "Devil Dog", and made a futile attempt to corral her. It was to no avail, as she disappeared into the woods with her accomplice close behind her. I was able to collar Squire because he did not have the power of evasive tactics, but he also did not have any of the stolen property in his jaws. Then Jim and I started to laugh, and knew right away that they had pulled a fast one on us, and maybe we were lucky that they only got away with a relatively small amount of what was supposed to be at least ten or 12 fresh venison dinners, for the human part of the family.

The next morning when I came down to let the dogs out for their morning run, and the venison had been put into the freezer, I looked sternly at Tonsils and Squire, and I'm sure that they both had the little smile that dogs exhibit when they know that they were a little bad, but not bad enough to be punished. Their slightly enlarged stomachs were proof that they had enjoyed the spoils of their sneak attack, and I am sure that there was not an ounce of remorse in either of them.

As the summer progressed, our minds were slowly able to put the experience of the fire behind us, No one had been injured and none of the children had even actually seen the active fire. It was difficult enough to witness the damage, but the sounds and the smells that accompany a fire of this magnitude, never leave your memory. Gwen and I still react to the sounds of fire whistles and sirens, differently than most individuals. We try not to even stay in anything higher than the fourth floor of any hotel that we visit. And even though my hearing is sub-par today, I can hear any sound that relates to the presence of fire even though my wife swears that I can't hear her when she has a "honey do suggestion." The slightest snap or crackle that I hear at any time raises my adrenalin level in the same way as the smell of any kind of smoke. I am sure that this reaction will stay with me all of my life!

This ability to be super sensitive to unusual abnormal sounds was proven again twelve years later when we were visiting Florida and staying in the condo of a friend. I awoke in the middle of the night to the faint, but recognizable, sound of the fire alarm. I awakened Gwen, and we started to investigate the rooms in the condo, and progressed to the hallway, where we could smell smoke. As the fire engines blared their way into our complex, we made our way down the fire escape stairs. Then we moved to the front of the building to see that one of the 32 units in the 4-story building was ablaze. It was on the second floor, and was a real inferno. Smoke curled up the outside of the building and flames licked the walls as the firefighters were starting their efforts to control it. It was a horrendous sight that was made worse by the fact that we knew who the owner of the condo was, and that there was absolutely nothing in the world that we could do to remedy the situation.

We knew the occupants and prayed they were not inside. It turned out that the husband had left the day before for a golf weekend, something that he had never done before. He rarely left her alone, but she was completely capable of managing on her own. The only factor that created a potential danger was that the middle-aged woman was addicted to smoking, and late-night reading. As it turned out, she had fallen asleep, with a lit cigarette near her chair, and the fire was out of control inside of a minute or two. She did not survive, and of course, he was heart broken. The construction of the building was such, that actually no damage of a major nature was suffered by any of the adjoining units. You would never have believed it was possible, if you had seen the blaze at its peak. The condo, which was on the Gulf of Mexico, turned out to become our winter home in later years, but we now had two dwellings that had had fire related experiences. We prayed that there would never be another!

The next few years were some of our more normal times. Tonsils and Squire kept providing us with joyful experiences, even the one that resulted in an interaction with a skunk that involved Tonsils, of course. She was a cute little dickens, but if trouble was around, she managed to find it, if not create it. She had a painful expression on her face, as we tried the age-old remedy of giving her a bath of tomato juice, which is not as easy as it sounds. The tomato juice would have better been used to make Bloody Marys, as it didn't have much of the desired effect of eliminating this distasteful odor. It was messy, and better results were achieved by the use of various dog friendly commercial shampoos. The only thing that could have been worse would have been an encounter with a porcupine.

A few months earlier, I had dropped into Dr. Jim's office one evening to find him working at his surgical table, lighted cigar (he always had one!) planted between his incisors, while he had an anaesthetized Beagle laid out in front of him. Jim hardly looked up as I approached, and looked at the poor dog that had made a big mistake in tangling with a fully armed and dangerous porcupine. But Beagles never seem to learn! Jim was using a special type of tweezers to extract quills that seemed to number somewhere between 50-75. No, porkies do not shoot them at you, but they smack you with their rear end, and you become the recipient of a quill sandwich. Hold the Mayo! Unfortunately for the puppy, the little spears were embedded in every part of his face, including his nose, and sadly, in one eye. He would recover with body intact except for lost vision in one eye, but the sad fact was he would not learn his lesson. This was already his second loss in two bouts with the "Prickly

Porkie." No Golden Retriever would ever exhibit a "Brain Cramp" like this little warrior endured.

It took him about an hour, and 90 percent of his cigar was consumed in the operation. Dr. Jim had a full veterinary practice, which meant that there were no types of animals that he would not treat. In one day, he might deliver a calf at 6 a.m., inseminate a cow, declaw a cat, spay or neuter a dog, cure a kennel cough and finish the day with a "Quillectomy." I never did see him do a tracheotomy on a Boa Constrictor, but I am sure that he could have done it! He did this for most of his life, except for Wednesday afternoons, when we always played golf in the summer and Paddle Tennis in the winter. Such was the life of this half of the "Hoof and Mouth Team."

As the seasons in Vermont rolled by, we understood why the state had a small but loyal population. Winter was sometimes harsh, but more often had its crisp, clean air free of pollution, and the joys of all types of outdoor healthy, recreational activities. All four children grew to be very competent ice skaters, and down hill skiers. Gwen even taught children at the local ski area, while I pretty much hung up the poles and barrel staves just shortly after I broke one wooden ski in half while executing a triple reverse, backwards double somersault, when I only meant to do a simple snow plow turn to avoid a large tree.

Now that I had a legitimate excuse for not joining the family on weekend skiing escapades, while at the same time extending my life expectancy, I could seek another outdoor winter activity. This was accomplished when some of our real died in the wool, native Vermonters (sometimes called Vermonsters), invited Gwen and me to an adult snow sliding party. Tobogganing is sometimes called traversing. This involved being together with about 10-12 hardy people, who were not averse to public drinking, and carousing, and saw no danger involved in flying down an icy back country road on a 10 foot long thin slab of wood, with no seat belts or air bags for protection, and steered only by a small section of rope. This group was in the age range of 35-50 with a undetermined IQ range. Common sense had yet to be invented, so it never came into play with this bunch!

Then each time we arrived at the bottom of the one half mile slope, more sturdy souls were waiting with the jeep and Styrofoam cups which seemed to be full of a pain killing fluid that did make things seem rosier. The temperature usually was 20 above to zero at night. They would wait until the other sleds found their place at ground zero, and we would drive up to the top again, for another try down the same slippery slope. Fortunately this was a road that was practically impassable for normal vehicles, and consequently we had no traffic at any time.

This went on for a few action-packed hours, until one of my real buddies, Bob Lewis, said, "how about if we try to go down on the snow packed open area of the adjacent pasture, we will be able to go much faster!" With our slightly altered sense of our own abilities, and being real men, six of us decided to abandon the simple path of the slick road, and try a new unknown trail to oblivion.

We jumped on to this slab of wood, with its waxed bottom, and proceeded to slowly run over the crusted snow. I was behind the man who was supposed to be steering, and I held a flashlight so that we had at least an inkling of what lay in our path. We picked up speed quickly with all six of us still on the flying object, heading for who knows where? As we approached top speed, I spotted a couple of what appeared to be just black horizontal lines, that turned out to be a nasty, rusty, barbed wire fence, which created an impassable object for our now, out of control missile. I think that I heard one passenger holler, "May Day, May Day!" but I dismissed that as a symbol of his inebriated condition, as we all knew that it was February!

All at once, there were six already partially numb adult men scattered over the snow blanket, fortunately only the gentleman who suggested this trip, seemed to be in some form of pain, and we carefully moved him and the sled back to the road, and with the others, headed for the nearest emergency room. He had suffered no broken bones, but we all decided it was time to return to his home, and enjoy the food that the giggling wives had prepared for us. This is one of the ways that makes all winters much easier to bear.

The winter season ended unhappily, as a new meaning of "de-ja vu" took place, when one morning I found our dear little Tonsils lying on the same floor as her mother Missy had, two years earlier. She had died painlessly from a heart attack at age 10 almost helping to prove that genes do play a large part in our lives. We would miss her terribly, because even though she was of small stature, she had a large heart that poured love into all of our lives. Now only Squire remained of what was not long ago an amazing canine "trio of joy and devotion." We take our beloved dogs for granted, and don't really realize how much love that they impart to us during their somewhat short lives. This is sometimes what makes the loss of one of these wonderful pets almost too much to bear for some folks, making it difficult for them to go through that sad experience again. With our family each loss was mourned and accepted, but nothing would ever make us not want to have a new experience that would come with another Golden puppy. We would start looking immediately for another one to keep "My 50 Golden Years" on track.

Squire
10/81

CHAPTER 11

Party Dog

Now that Squire was our only pet, he seemed lonely at times, and kept looking around to find one of his old friends. This probably accounts for the manner in which he now behaved. He was always quiet, and less frisky than the others, but he would not let us out of his sight. He always parked himself between one of us and the back door, so that there was no way to leave the house without him. He was always at the side of whoever was home at the time, and moved from room to room as a shadow, whenever we changed locations. I had to cringe sometimes when he would struggle to move his weakened hips to get up when I was only going to go a short distance. When he reached his new destination as near to you as he could manage, he would plop himself down like a sack of bones with a resounding thump and the look of accomplishment that comes from taking the weight off of his tired legs.

Once in a while I was able to get off to the golf course, and every time we reached the 7th hole at the Woodstock golf course, there was a Golden, that lived next to the golf course. He always wore a big red ribbon, and roamed around this particular hole. The hole was a par three, played over a large pond, which covered most of the space between the elevated tee and the green itself. I never found out his name, but as we approached the tee for our attempt at reaching the putting surface, he plopped himself right in the center of the two foot deep pond. He would sit facing us, when we were 160 yards away, and waited eagerly for one of us to have a bad shot. He knew us better than we thought, as one out of the five or six shots would invariably splash into the pond, whereupon he would swim directly to the ball, and actually retrieve it, and drop it at the edge of the pond. I was sometimes fearful that one of those errant shots would bean him, but it never happened.

After every retrieval, he would station himself back to the middle of the pond to await the next group. His behavior prompted me to bring a few of my young boys, down to the pond in the evening, and in their bathing suits, would pick 50-100 golf balls from the murky water. The Golden Retriever did not bother with those that were already at the bottom of the pond. They would be saved for us. This operation kept the whole family in golf balls, as we would never think of selling any of the little white treasures. Did you know that golf balls sold in a Pro shop can go as high as $4.00 per ball?

When fall arrived, we looked forward to our final days of fall foliage golf, and since the Vermont deer season was open at the same time, Dr. Jim and I decided to have a little fun at the expense of our very young golf pro. It was normal procedure to pull our heavy golf bags on a golf pull cart, as it provided more exercise than riding an electric contraption. One Thanksgiving Day, which always came at the end of the November Deer Season, as part of our plan and celebration of the traditional holiday, Dr. Jim and I brought our deer rifles to the parking lot of the Country Club, and then placed them barrel end down into the midst of the golf clubs. It was a tight fit, but we managed to have them stay in amongst the other clubs. Did anyone ever hear of a 30-30 or 30-06 iron? This was going to be a first in golf, at least for this Club, even though I have played other courses that had deer running all over the place. If we had ever pulled out these weapons on the fairways however, you would have seen people also running all over the same place!

As we both marched nonchalantly past the entrance to the pro shop, and towards the first teé, the young pro and his cute wife met us with a smile and a nice Thanksgiving greeting. It was not until we were halfway to the teeing area, that they both noticed the butt end of our deer rifles sticking out of the golf bags. At first they were speechless, but the pro finally stammered, "Are those real guns?" We looked at him, and with straight faces replied, "Yes of course, why else would we be wearing our Blaze Orange hunting caps?" The young pro then said "But you can't hunt on the golf course!" We replied, "Why not, there are no "No Hunting" signs posted, and we are both excellent marksmen. Everyone knows that you shoot "Birdies" on the course all of the time, so why not deer??"

Then I said, "Haven't you seen the damage that these deer have inflicted on the golf course. There are hoof prints in all of the sand traps, and there are droppings on the greens, plus they are eating all of the beautiful flowers, they must be eliminated". Of course neither of us really dreamed of shooting any deer on the golf course, but we played it out for as long as we could. About this time, the poor young couple did not know whether to call the police or just hope that no deer showed up that day. I don't think that they would ever be faced again with a comparable situation to this in their entire careers! They had just experienced the fun side of the "Hoof and Mouth Team!"

As we grew older, the winter season seemed to have less appeal, and although we were not ready to retire as yet, the thought of warm weather began to get more interesting. The four kids were now all attending different schools, and as spring sprung upon us, we usually had a party that would bring a variety of kids to our annual "Butz Bash." This was a two-day affair, and the rules were carefully outlined and understood by all. No one would be allowed to leave before the breakfast meal on the second day. There would be nobody driving on the night of the main party. Since we had a sizable lawn, we did allow some of the kids to pitch tents around the pool. Food was cooked by the guys and girls who had proven their ability to furnish meals that would not give anyone ptomaine poisoning. The guests were aged 18-22, and policed themselves when it came to decisions about coke or beer. There was no hard liquor available. The young adults would make sure that no abuses occurred, because they knew that they would not see another "Bash", if the rules were violated.

On the deck we had tables full of snacks that surrounded a smaller table with a large keg of beer. This "Fountain of Youth" had an overflow tray that accumulated the beer that spilled as glasses were filled. Squire, our canine beertender was getting his share of love and attention from 20-30 people, and you could see that he enjoyed that. One problem was that he was also getting his share of overflow beer as he passed the keg. Of course, he had no idea that this was not his normal water dish, and with some encouragement from the spectators, he returned more than once. Even though he was a large dog, it was only a matter of time before he started to react to the mild intoxicant. He didn't fall off the deck, but I had to shut him down, when some of the revelers tried to get him to jump off of the diving board. I brought the party animal back into the house so that he could sleep it off on his doggy bed. He had had his fill of college life even though few dogs die of cirrhosis of the liver.

All in all, this party was always a success, and was continued until all of the kids had graduated from college. I must say however, these parties were 22-25 years ago, and with the culture changes that I have observed lately, this type of responsible activity would be difficult to pull off again. We had no drug problems to contend with that we were aware of, but I am not entirely sure of that either!

Before we allowed any of the revelers to depart on the morning of the second day, they all had breakfast, and everyone helped clean up the property, so that no one would ever think a "Bash", had occurred. Even Squire swore that he really did not have too much, when he awoke from his deep slumber. It was refreshing to have a group of college students that could have a good time, without any of them creating a problem of any nature. After enjoying the camaraderie, every one went their merry way, and we returned to our relatively normal way of life. The dog would have been quite content with a party every day, since he was the recipient of a month's worth of petting and exercise, as the young people had strong arms and a willingness to participate in almost endless toss and retrieve games. The beer probably helped him cope with his painful hips, and I am sure that many humans use this same excuse for self-medicating their aching bones.

Squire was a fairly quiet old boy, and had already begun to start the gray or whitening process, that turned his face, in particular, into a picture of grandeur and nobility. His large brown eyes could still convey his love for us, and his body was also beginning to shows some signs of aging. His hip dysplasia was already causing mobility problems, but as yet, he exhibited no signs of pain, or discomfort. I am sure that he would try to never show the presence of pain, and we reciprocated, by not participating in any activity that would result in any type of injuries. He was content to lie in front of the fireplace, and to go outside for short walks with us as long as the temperature was above zero. I don't think that even the sudden appearance of a bunny would stir him to cut to the chase!

Vermont has a climate that because of the relative lack of humidity makes it possible to participate in many outdoor activities that would not be tolerable with high moisture content. One sport that we enjoyed in winter, besides skiing and skating, is paddle tennis. The metal court with 10 foot high chicken wire fencing on all 4 sides that is used in the game has the capability of being heated by propane heaters so that even heavy snow melts on contact with the surface, and does not inhibit play. The only thing that really puts a crimp into our ability to play is the fact that the ball used in the game is made of a solid rubber like material that loses its resilience as the temperature drops. The ball will bounce about two to three feet high at 70 degrees, but when the thermometer reaches zero degrees, the little sphere will manage only a three-inch bounce. Did you ever try to hit a rock hard ball that only was bouncing above your toe line?

When it's really cold, that is when the real fun begins, as we adjourn to the little hut adjacent to the court that has the wood fire stove. There are always some folks who have the foresight to bring a picnic, and the beverages that prevent severe cases of frostbite. Although a bit of Scotch whisky does wonders for the players, there has been no significant evidence to prove that even total immersion of the ball in 80-proof liquid will bring it back to its original bounceabilty. But, by then who cares?

When the food and drink options have been exhausted, it is usually time to go home, since further play would probably be fruitless, even if a new warm ball could be found. The older used paddle balls are then, of course turned over to the folks who are fortunate enough to have a dog waiting faithfully by your home fireplace wondering why in the world would anyone ever want to go out into that type of frigid weather? There were many times when I also was of the same opinion.

As the winter forged on, and the first signs of spring arrived, Gwen and I began to think that it was getting to the stage that Squire needed a new four legged friend to keep him running and thereby lengthening his life expectancy. He was already older than all of our previous retrievers had been, and our observations seemed to indicate that 10-12 years was a good average life span for a Golden Retriever. When his partial disability was added to the equation, it was easy to see that another puppy would be necessary to continue my string of "Golden Years", which had now covered 30 years from 1956 to 1986. I needed to give some sincere thought relative to the acquisition of a new puppy for Squire and the family.

One thing worried me about the arrival on the scene of a new puppy, and it involved a very sad incident that occurred in our town a few years ago. A family that I knew, had an old dog similar in age to our Squire, and with a personality that I thought was normal to all Golden Retrievers. Not!! This dog had shown no signs of mean behavior, at any time, and was a good family pet. Because of his age, this family decided to bring a new puppy into their home, feeling that this would be a positive experience for all concerned. Unfortunately, the end result was quite sad, when the new pup was introduced to this elder dog, the old boy attacked the puppy, biting his neck and violently shaking the young dog in a way that caused the immediate demise of the newcomer. A terrible display of envy and dislike resulted in this unexplainable act of violence. Everyone was terribly shocked, and saddened by the event, and its effect on all that were involved. It was proof positive that animals like humans, do not always fit the same mold. Although I was not present at this event, I never heard of this type of behavior, either before or since. It did however make me a little cautious about our upcoming reunion with Squire and his new companion.

Now here I was about to introduce, in a like manner, a new dog into an uncomfortably similar situation. The question flashed through my mind about the advisability of what I was about to do. I was sure that no other Golden would ever do that. "Would he or she??" At least, I knew that I would have to be very cautious, and patient when and if such a union would take place at my home. With this in mind, I decided that it would work, so the die was cast.

CHAPTER 12

A Prince of a Dog

On the 15th of September 1985, I was working in the office even though it was my birthday (hardly a reason to take off from work!). Dentistry is one of many professions in which we get paid only if you do something. In my day you didn't get any remuneration for just talking, or looking, since a task of some sort was expected to be completed. In other words, you had to straighten a child's teeth, or you repaired one, or any of the other operations that we do in order to expect a payment for services. There was no such a procedure, as talking about what we intended to do. This is not necessarily true today, as a fee is usually charged for almost anything that happens in the office in todays' world.

Our new office had tile floors to ease maintenance, and thus a slightly slippery floor was provided that made it difficult for a puppy, for instance to gain traction. This fact was soon to be proven true, as my wife entered my office unannounced, and from behind me plunked a large woven basket down on the floor, next to where I sat on my swivel stool. She happily said "Happy Birthday Dear," as she pulled a light blanket off of the top of the container, and revealed a golden, fuzzy pile of pure joy also known as a Golden Retriever baby. She removed him from the basket and placed him on the floor next to me, whereupon the poor little guy could not get his footing, and all four paws splayed out in different directions, as his little belly touched down on the slippery surface. I am not sure who was more surprised, the puppy or me! His cute little tail was wagging furiously, even though he was not sure what he was supposed to be doing.

I scooped him up in my arms, and received my first puppy kiss from a new little critter, soon to be named Prince or Princee One. It was a wonderful surprise, and a joyous event, but I am not sure what my patients' reaction was to be, but who could resist a Golden puppy?? Just so long as he did not whittle on my waiting room carpet.

Since I had to continue working with my patient, and would have to wait until later to fully enjoy my new birthday gift, Gwen gathered Prince back into the basket, and left quietly to return home. However, this little surprise visit was to become another ingot in my 50 Golden Year collection!

After I rushed home, following Gwen with the puppy, I was thinking about how I was going to affect the meeting of puppy Prince and the Squire of Pine View. Would it be happy and harmonious, or could there be trouble brewing? I took a positive mental approach, as I took the dog out of his basket and walked toward "Good old Squire". He gazed nonchalantly at this new intruder as if to say, "What's the big deal?" and walked towards the house door. I set Prince down on the ground whereupon the little guy made a wobbly beeline for the big old dog standing in front of him. I held the puppy while Squire eyed him and started to sniff around the new arrival, checking out all parts until he was assured that this was not any aggressor, and I was able to feel that all would be okay, and it was. It was quite a scene to behold as Squire even with his weak rear end was towering over his new little buddy, who was now wagging his little tail feverishly as he looked to gain favor from this monster old boy that he had just met.

We all went into the house, and Squire went over to a small blanket in front of the fireplace, that was his own special place. He lay down as was his custom, and to my surprise lay quietly in place as his new little buddy approached, and promptly curled up inside Squires' large paws as if he had always been there, and deserved to be there. What a relief that this was going to be better than I ever expected, and I wondered why I ever thought it would be a problem.

One of the reasons Squire lived to be the oldest Golden that I ever had, was due in large part to the exercise that he derived from cavorting with the young Prince, who at that time was tireless. Poor Squire with his weak hindquarters was no match for the puppy, even though he was a larger than average Golden. He had long legs, but they did not always work together. Both dogs loved to race around the yard, and showed no inclination to chase the ever-present deer, or to roam into the woods, which were plentiful.

Squire did not have the endurance to chase after any female scents, as our former dog Tawny, did, and Prince lost his interest in the opposite sex for an entirely different reason. While he was still less than a year old, he was unable to retain his food one day which is of course, most unusual for any young dog. So after two days of being not able to keep the tasty nuggets in the proper digestive area, I had to call good old Dr. Roberts for advice. Of course, Jim asked me to bring over the patient who by now had lost a great deal of his normal vim and vitality. As Jim examined him, he came up with two conclusions, since he did not have state-of-the-art radiology equipment, or any X-ray at all. His conclusions were, first, that he had been poisoned, or second, that he had some blockage that could not be pinpointed with any accuracy without the aforementioned equipment. Therefore, he referred me to a young Veterinarian in the next town, about 30 miles away who had the necessary diagnostic tools.

So, I bundled the unhappy pup, and my now very nervous wife, into the station wagon and took off for the next exam. Then, after we were introduced to the new young veterinarian, he took our sick little guy off to the radiology section of his hospital, and we waited nervously in the waiting room as all anxious parents end up doing at some time in their lives. About thirty minutes later the Vet returned with a smile on his face that gave us some immediate relief, and then proceeded to show us a large X-ray film, that upon examination, showed him what the problem was. The radiographs that I was used to reading were, of course, quite small compared to the ones needed for larger animals, however I was at least better equipped than most folks to interpret the film.

The Vet took the film and placed it on the viewer that had a bright light behind it, and he proceeded to point out the causative agent, or object to us. At first glance we could see a perfectly round object about one and half inches in diameter that appeared to be lodged in the dogs stomach, and precluded any worry about poison as a problem. He then asked if we played golf at all, and we had to both plead guilty to that question. "What has golf got to do with this problem?" I asked. "Well, it seems as though your new little buddy has retrieved a golf ball from somewhere, and after chewing the outside cover off, decided to swallow the rest. "The rest," consisted of a hard rubber core that was just a bit smaller than the whole ball. It was large enough however, to completely block all of his digestive system, resulting in his inability to pass anything through. The good news was that it was a removable object. The decision was made to perform surgery to remove the ex Titleist ball, and while we were at it, he suggested, that it would be a perfect time to neuter our little boy since we had concluded that we would not have any more raging hormones roaming the premises. When the operation was completed, the Vet gave me the very expensive ball and the X-ray of it so that I could make a copy of it for our files.

At the time, I had a good friend, Dr. Jack McCutcheon who was the head of the radiology clinic at a nearby hospital, and had the ability to copy the X-rays easily. I asked him if he could make a copy of the film. When he returned with my 11 by 14 X-ray, it was fairly simple to visualize the round opaque object that had once flown over the turf at a local golf course. When I inquired of my friend what the cost of the copy would be, he wrote on the film with a wax pencil that is used to mark films, the following, "There will be no charge for this film, as you have already been penalized a stroke!" I then took the X-ray and the ball over to see Dr. Jim, whereupon we both had a good chuckle over the episode. It suddenly occurred to me that we probably had at least 100 similar golf balls scattered around our property, all of which had the potential of creating a generous pension fund for my friend Veterinarian. I hoped that Prince had learned his lesson, but you never know!

It took only a few days for Prince to adapt to his life as chief tormenter of his partially lame pal Squire. Prince recognized the fact that he was faster, and far more flexible than Squire, and he quickly took advantage of this knowledge. As it turned out, the constant chasing about was one of the real reasons that Squire lived to be 14 years old, and became the longest living dog of our 50 Golden Years.

As if to prove that Dr. Jim was really a normal human being, and not just a great Veterinarian, I want to relate the story about him that occurred in my office, and not in his. On this particular day, Dr. Jim called me at the Health Center, to see if I could see him right away. I of course, told him that he could come in immediately, just as he would do for me if the situations were reversed. At this time Jim was in his early 60s, and even with good dental care, I had to remove a tooth occasionally. In this case there was no avoiding the need for the extraction of his upper right second molar.

When he arrived, I could see that he was not having a good day, and even his sometimes gruff manner was quieted by his need for immediate pain relief. We had our usual give and take kidding, as we usually did, especially when playing golf, as he was an expert needler. When I told him with a straight face that most men would have this extraction performed without any pain relievers except for a few baby aspirins. Then I asked him if that was OK with him and he gave me the famous Hawaiian peace sign, or at least that was what I thought it was! His face grew into a more cheerful countenance as the anesthetic took hold and quickly alleviated his pain. Jim always had a cigar in his mouth, even while swinging a golf club, and sometimes it was lit, and more often he just chewed on it. One day when he arrived for a normal visit, he laid his still lit cigar on the instrument table on my right side, and then asked permission to leave it there, while I took care of his tooth. A security blanket, no doubt, and it did perform a secondary function of keeping away the mosquitoes. I don't think that many offices allowed that to happen in their smoke free zones, but we were after all good buddies, and it did make him feel more comfortable.

When the niceties and kidding around were over, I proceeded to remove the tooth with relative ease, at least from my point of view, and stuff a great wad of sterile cotton into his mouth to help stop the normal amount of bleeding that followed all extractions. Most of my patients usually remarked that I would always fill their oral cavity with humongous amounts of cotton pads, and then ask a question that required an answer involving more than just a nod or grunt. I think that all dentists are charged with that crime, since normally the dentist never loses an argument over anything as long as he has the patient's mouth open, and a handful of cotton pads, or even a few fingers inserted therein. This is a great time to express any wacko political commentary, without worrying about an adverse opinion interfering with your normal logical explanation of how the world should be run!

Now that the offending tooth was gone, I thought it safe to show him the three rooted object, slightly covered with blood, and to prove that I had performed pretty well since he had never uttered a sound during the procedure. The moment he saw the molar that had resided in his mouth for the last 50 plus years, he slumped down in the chair, and temporarily lost consciousness. Fortunately, most dental chairs are somewhat reclining anyhow, and all I had to do was to apply oxygen through the mask located on the wall beside him, and in a matter of a few seconds, he was back with us.

It was a good chance for me to get back at some of the ribbing that he had inflicted on me over the years. I said to him "You big sissy, after all of the blood and gore associated with a real veterinary practice, how could you faint?" "Well," he said, "it's completely different when it is your blood, now give me my cigar back." The office staff politely snickered over this as he left the office with gauze protruding from one side of his mouth, and his still lit cigar hanging out of the opposite side. The office remained mosquito free for several years after his cigar smoke treatment and we all thanked him for that.

Strange as it may seem, I had a quite similar experience with a young man in our small town that had quite a reputation for being a very tough guy when fighting anyone after he had a few too many drinks. We were always friends, and when he had a fight that removed one-third of a tooth, he came to me to have the remaining section of root removed. Once again, I had underestimated the situation, and without thinking, showed him the remains of his tooth after removing it, whereupon he pulled another "Pass out act", just as Dr. Jim had. I vowed at that time that I would only show an extracted tooth again to a little old lady after the fact, because I was sure that she could handle this minor trauma better than any big tough male person.

Prince 1986

Gwen—Jack—Prince
1987

Jack—Prince—Squire

CHAPTER 13

A Cautionary Tale

One of life's lessons involving how to train and raise a puppy occurred one day in the spring, and involved the brand new young male Prince and our older more experienced old boy Squire. They were, of course wonderful companions to each other, and were constantly having play dog-fights. I am sure that most dogs enjoy these encounters, as they growl and snarl at each other, while trying to grab a leg or attack each other's throats. This is completely natural, and no malice is meant or shown by this behavior, as they are really having a lot of fun. I am not sure why a Golden Retriever plays this way, since I have never observed a Golden intentionally attacking a human being. However, a female friend told me that she was involved in an incident in downtown Tampa Florida, where her female Golden Retriever attacked, and actually bit a man that attempted to reach in the driver's side window and injure her owner. The dog was able to bite the neck of the intruder who dropped to the street, as the frightened woman drove off away from the scene of a potentially serious situation. I bet that that guy never tried that stunt again, at least not with a dog in the car!

However, training is of such importance to the relationship that any dog and its owner will have, and since I have not owned any other breed of dog except Goldens for fifty years, I cannot speak for all of the other breeds in the world. Perhaps all dogs have the innate intelligence and good behavior patterns that are exhibited by Goldens, but I doubt it. If you are an owner of this breed, I really do not have to go on about their virtues, but if you are in the process of picking out your first new canine companion, you might be sorry if you did not have an interview with at least one of the retriever class of dogs.

During Prince's early life I had spent a good deal of time training him with a choke chain and leash. The choke chain has some good advantages as a learning tool, however each owner must also be cognizant of the dangers associated with this tool. It isn't called a "choke chain" for nothing because it mainly works because it temporarily can choke your pet. There have been unfortunate cases when a dog has been injured seriously, or even killed when its chain was caught by accident in a fence or on a tree branch, when the owner was not in the immediate vicinity.

One lovely Vermont spring afternoon when Prince was a fully-grown handsome male, he was in a very playful mood, teasing and bullying his older pal Squire, when something happened that nearly changed his life, as well as ours. I was upstairs on the second floor of our Colonial home, when I heard what seemed to me to be an unusual type of barking, and growling from the large 1ˢᵗ floor back deck that led down to the backyard and swimming pool area. Even though the boys were always tussling with each other, this time the barking had a different, almost ominous sound to it, so I rushed down the stairs, and through the family room to the door that fronted on the deck.

At first, all I saw was the two dogs in a pile of golden fur that was not that unusual, but was somehow different. As I reached down towards the heads that seemed almost interlocked, I couldn't believe my eyes as I quickly saw that the chain around Prince's neck was so tight that I could not even get a finger under it. By a freak of nature, Squire had gotten his mouth opened in such a position that his 2 lower large canine teeth had locked under the chain, and when Prince, in an escape maneuver flipped over, the choke chain was immediately tightened to the point, that his escape was impossible, and he was fast losing the ability to breath. Since I could see that the chain was too tight to undo by hand, I dashed down the cellar steps to my basement work-room, to get a hack saw, since I had no tool as a bolt cutter. The saw would do if I had enough time, but did I?? At about the same moment, my daughter Debby, who was home from school, had heard the racket from her upstairs bedroom, and we almost ran into each other as we both rushed to the deck.

By the grace of God, Prince had flipped his body back again over Squires head in such a way as to release the death grip. The poor puppy had already urinated and defecated on the deck, which is a common reaction of humans and animals that are near death, and are losing their ability to control these functions. Talk about a near death experience, this was certainly one for the Prince. Cats may have nine lives however, there is no folklore like that associated with the canine culture. As I reached down, and put my arms around Prince to see that he was still breathing, I was able to unhook the chain that was still caught in Squires' canine teeth. The poor big dog had no clue what had just happened, and I will never know if I would have been able to cut the chain.

It was then that the thought occurred to me, what a horrible event it might have been, if no one had been home to at least assist in the miracle. It took two or three days before Prince was completely normal, and all he could do for a day was to lie quietly on his bed, never really knowing what could have been the result of his seemingly innocent play combat with his pal. So if this little story about the dangers involved with choke chain collars doesn't provide food for thought, at least I tried. As you can imagine, we no longer have any choke chains on the property and suggest that perhaps no one should use them except with grossly misbehaving grandchildren or mother's-in-law. (Only kidding of course!)

The two dogs enjoyed this summer and fall in Vermont, much the same way as the rest of the family. The children were all home from school, and involved themselves in the various activities that Vermont provides. The weather in the summer can be everything from 60 to 100 degrees, with periods of dryness interspersed with 2-3 rainy days.

My children were all involved in various sorts of summer jobs that ranged from bartending and cooking at a local hotel, to landscape chores at the nearby Laurance Rockefeller mansion. When there was any time available, the boys would help me to perform the property maintenance necessary to take care of our seven acres of land, which was mostly filled with pine trees and aptly named "Pine View." Since the dogs had no training in manual arts, they were relegated to perform as "Watch Dogs" and deer chasers. A job which they thoroughly enjoyed, and had very good performance ratings attached thereto. It was usually my job to perform the somewhat dangerous tasks, such as the trimming and thinning of trees, in order to improve the view, as well as for the health of the mini forest. When all of the helpers went back to school, I was just pulling my Jeep into the garage after work, when I noticed that one of the pine trees had grown enough to be impinging on the roof of my tool shed. Since the day had been a little stressful, I went into the house to change clothes in order to do some work of the manual variety outside of the house. Even though I used my hands in everyday work I was always happy when I could repair or renovate something around the property.

But first, I prepared a Manhattan cocktail as was my habit, before enjoying one of my wife's wonderful dinners. After I had thoughtfully consumed about one-third of the concoction, it occurred to me that the tree that I had just observed really needed to be tended to. I strolled through the kitchen casually, drink in hand, and headed out for the work-bench that was located in the garage. The one half glass of Manhattan was placed on a shelf as I reached for a step ladder and a small chain saw, and marched toward the targeted pine trees. I managed to lean the ladder against the front of the slightly inclined roof, and with the chain saw in one hand I mounted the 6-7 rungs of the ladder. When I safely reached the asphalt shingle roof I quickly pulled the ladder up onto the 8-foot tall shack, and proceeded to place it up against the tree trunk. Even though it was a bit unwieldy, I managed to climb about four steps up the incline with the trusty mechanical blade in one hand until I was sure that I could reach the desired level for the cut. It was then that a thought flashed through my cerebrum that said to me "Why are you doing this??" In a matter of seconds, I dismissed the warning, and started up the saw. Of course the dumb thing wouldn't start up right away as it always did when on ground level, so I had to dismount to the shed roof to get the thing to run. There are some advantages to plain old regular tools!

One advantage that a small chain saw has is that it is easy to run with one hand. Another advantage is that the blade is only 12 inches long, and in case of an accident would probably only remove a few fingers, and not a complete arm. Since I was the recipient of only one half of an alcoholic liquid, I was even more sure of my competence to handle this simple chore. I was almost through with the cut on the tree, when my wife approached, after hearing the loud sound of the whirring blade, and screamed at me in a somewhat restrained manner, the same phrase that my mind had uttered only a few minutes earlier. "Why are you doing this, have you been drinking??"

Just as she finished her reprimand, the spiffy little saw completed its job, and the top of the tree fell perfectly to the ground. By this time, even Prince and Squire had arrived on the scene, both of them looking up at me with puzzled expressions, did they also know that their Dad had done a foolish thing? I retreated meekly down the ladder to the roof, and lowered the ladder to the ground, and walked with it and the saw to the garage. In a clever move, I decided to leave the half full glass in the garage, and took my wife's hand as we returned to the kitchen. I remarked that it was not really a dangerous job, so why don't we just have a before dinner cocktail. She agreed, and I decided that I would let well enough alone, and promised myself to relate the complete story to the three boys later as a "Do as I say, not as I do" story. Needless to say that was the last one-handed chainsaw act that was ever seen at "Pine View". I later heard that an act similar to it was seen at "Cirque du Soleil"

It was just shortly after that when we noticed that Squire was having a very difficult time trying to run with Prince, and his breathing was heavy without much exertion. He was now fourteen years old, and none of my previous Goldens had achieved that goal, made even more remarkable with his long-term bout with hip dysplasia.

The next morning, I took him to see Dr. Jim, and he agreed to keep him overnight. Later in that day he called me to tell me that Squire would not make it much longer as his heart was giving out, and this situation was complicated by kidney breakdown. That meant his time with us was ending. Although I had made it through the demise of four Goldens over the years with no shed tears, it was still difficult to ask him to please take care of every thing, as he always did in such a professional manner. We notified all of the children, and wondered how Prince would react to his absence. We of course, have no way of knowing exactly how one dog understands the loss of a litter mate or any other dog that they may have spent time with. Their perceptions are unknown to us, but we like to think that these creatures feel happiness, love, pain and death in much the same way as we do as humans.

We knew that we were now the only family that Prince had, and we also knew that we would all try to love him even more than before. It did seem that Prince would try to keep one of us in his sight at all times, even moving from room to room with us as we performed various duties around the house. Someone, who had a Golden for many years, suggested that all of these loving dogs should be named "Velcro," reflecting their tendency to always be close to it's friends, and to maintain some physical contact at all times. All of my dogs had been "Leaners, and whenever there was an opportunity to snuggle up against anyone, they would. This was a far more socially accepted behavioral act than "Humping" a leg!"

A few months after the death of our senior citizen Squire, I left the house in a small snowstorm that had dropped 4-6 inches of that beautiful white fluff, covering the landscape, and making everything look the same, but all white. One of my summer neighbors had departed for Florida and had asked me to "Baby Sit" his beautiful home for the winter. The house was at the end of a one quarter mile gravel road whose incline made it quite difficult to traverse excepting with a four wheel drive vehicle, and even then it could be rendered impossible with only a little ice cover. Every few days I would climb up the hill to make sure that there were no plumbing problems, roof leaks, or other signs of mischief of any kind. Fortunately, in Vermont, we do not have many house break-ins even now. When I had left the house, I did not see any sign of Prince even though I knew that he was in the house somewhere, probably near a fireplace, one of which was usually burning split wood logs into warmth that is difficult to match, even with an oil furnace. The maple and oak logs also give off a wondrous aroma that remains in the house, and is much more user-friendly than the scent of fuel oil.

As I climbed the hill by myself, I observed the beauty of the fresh snow accumulating on the pine boughs, with little frisky Red squirrels racing from place to place. It was so quiet and peaceful, and is a good reason why many people, (even retired} still continue to live in and enjoy the wonders of a Vermont winter. When I unlocked the front door, and entered the beautiful butternut walled foyer, everything appeared normal. As I entered the kitchen a strange sight hit me, as I noticed that there were many varied objects strewn over the floor, and the kitchen counters. There were pinecones, acorns, kitchen utensils, and others small knick-knacks everywhere. At first I thought that one of my friends' children might have visited and ended up with a food fight, or other strange behavior.

As I moved around the living room, I didn't notice any signs of forced entry, but the wood around the windows had been ripped as though by a knife or claws of some kind. It was then, that I heard a muffled bark coming from outside the front door, and when I opened it, in popped my buddy Prince, with his tail wagging, as if to proudly announce to me that he could track me even over a snow covered road that he did not even see me enter. I had always heard stories about the wonderful sense of smell that dogs have, especially hunting dogs, but this was proof positive. Now here he was, and just in time to help me find out whatever, or whoever had created the mess that I encountered in the kitchen. Suddenly, Prince bolted towards the large living room that included an immense stone fireplace, and headed for the draperies that covered the entire wall. He barked as if to say, "Come on Dad, can't you see that large squirrel atop the drapes?" sure enough, that began the unbelievably fast chase around the room, with me coming in last with a heavy broom as my choice of weapons. Prince bounded after the squirrel, which dashed into the adjoining large master bedroom, where he disappeared. I could not see it but I knew at least what it was and where it was, and I could now isolate it to one room. I closed the door, and returned to the kitchen while Prince guarded the now closed door, and we had at least succeeded in trapping him into one smaller location.

It was soon apparent that the squirrel had come down the open flue of the fireplace, and could not get back up the slippery sides of the chimney. So it started to attack the window and door frames, causing damage later estimated at $2000 dollars. It had attacked the dried arrangements of nuts and pine cones for food, since the poor squirrel was probably in the house for a few days, it tried to claw its way out through the window casings, and actually had made good progress. I was relieved that no human had inflicted this amazing amount of damage, and now Prince and I had to finish the job. I decided that the room was too large to search into every nook and cranny, so we left the house to return the next morning. The two of us walked back down the snow-covered lane, and I at least had a different feeling about how cute those little destructive squirrels actually were.

In the morning my pal was eager to return to the lair of the dreaded rodent, in order to retaliate. I carried a fish net and a lacrosse stick now that I had seen proof of the results that the squirrel can achieve using teeth and razor sharp claws. As I opened the bedroom door, and looked at the threshold, I could see where the little trapped devil had chewed and clawed a large section of the carpet up in a vain attempt to escape. Now where to look was the question, since it is hard to think like a squirrel, but I had a secret weapon in the form of a big, ferocious, red dog named Prince. The first thing that I noticed that looked out of place to me was a little mound in the middle of the king size bed, that lay under the covers. Now that I was sure that our perpetrator was located, I went to the far wall to open up the drapes, and the sliding doors that provided an easy access out into the wooded area outside. At first, I pondered how hard I wanted to whack the lump however, I really did not want to make a mess on the underlying sheets, and I did not want Prince to risk injury at the hands or claws of this nasty adversary.

Instead of whacking him with the lacrosse stick, I picked up an empty metal trash basket, and bopped the unsuspecting hump making a fairly loud sound, but inflicting little damage to the bed coverings. In a flash, the object of this attack scurried out from under the covers, and made a speedy dash across the floor, and even went out the door that I had opened beforehand. It happened so fast that Prince hardly moved, and when he realized how far the squirrel had already gone in large bounds, he just wagged his tail while I laughed at this silly situation. The lesson involved here for those with fireplaces is simple; never leave the house with an open flue, no matter what the size of the chimney, or the time of the year.

With mission accomplished, I gathered up the assorted tools and returned home so I could call my friend in Florida and give him a blow-by-blow account of the entire procedure. He would return in the spring to repair the damage, and perhaps reward Prince with a box of Dog treats. It took him a long time to really believe that a small rodent that looks so innocent could have created that much destruction. This story perhaps explains why more people have dogs as pets and not squirrels!!

CHAPTER 14

Heading South

In late 1986, a family decision was made that would change our lives drastically. Because of the premature death by heart attack, of my father at the age of 46, I had given a lot of consideration to a reasonably early retirement. The four children were now out of college, and they were already on the way to various careers. For some unknown reason, I felt that my genes would perhaps cause me to have a shorter life span than normal, so maybe my wife and our Golden should endeavor to start a new life that meant a part-time move to a warmer climate like Florida. Vermont would be wonderful for the summer and fall, but the sunshine would be beckoning us for the winter and spring. Gwen and I both enjoyed golf and tennis, so that it was easy to spend at least half of the year near the water and warm weather that Florida offered. Prince, of course had no clue about what a partial move might involve, and as long as he was near us, there was no problem for him.

In 1979, in anticipation of a Florida move, we had purchased a small condo on the west coast called Innisbrook Golf Resort. This was where we had decided to move to, however we felt that if we were looking for a water view, we needed to have a larger two-bedroom condo that was not too far away from our golf course. It was our great fortune to find a third floor condo overlooking the Gulf of Mexico, in the small town of Tarpon Springs, Florida. This town is predominantly a Greek fishing village with a great deal of charm. The Greek folks that live here are still very active in the catching of shrimp, scallops, grouper, mullet and the still dangerous task of deep sea diving for sponges that are still considered better than any artificial substitute. Prince enjoyed the new location because he could sit on our porch and observe the activity on the water provided by fishing boats, leaping mullet and the occasional visit by a school of Dolphins.

We were moved in for about a month when we began to notice that two or three young men were residing in the condo directly above us on the fourth floor. This was the top floor, and rendered a beautiful panoramic view to the south and west over the Gulf of Mexico. Our building was only about 20 yards from the edge of the water where I later kept my small mini-whaler boat.

It seemed a little strange that the young men were gone most of the time, and when they did arrive at the condo they drove two exceedingly expensive automobiles. One was a Porsche convertible and the other an even more expensive

European car that looked to me like a Lamborghini. The boys kept very much to themselves and I never did get to talk with any of them.

Just below their condo was a small peninsula of land that stretched about 30 yards out into the water. It was covered with mangrove bushes with one or two spindly trees out at the tip. It was very dense and difficult to walk to, but when the tide went out it was easily accessible. One day as I looked out over the beautiful water I noticed two colored balloons were attached to the little trees and were floating a few feet above the tops of the trees. It was puzzling to me how they ever got there, but it was obvious that someone had placed them there.

The very next day as I sat on my deck, a very old seaplane that was completely unmarked, swooped down low enough that I could see a pilot. This seemed also to be rather extraordinary, and then it became a regular occurrence as it came by the same way every few days.

While all of this was happening, there was a large drug bust in Tarpon Springs, Florida, where drugs were discovered inside of hollowed out logs that were brought in by boat. Suddenly it struck me that the sudden appearance of signal balloons on the trees adjacent to where the boys lived, the low flying seaplane and the fancy cars that they drove must be all tied in together. It was a perfect place to make shipments of illegal drugs without being detected.

Since I did not have any proof, and was not a law enforcement officer, I did not report these incidents to anyone. After a few months we were to return to Vermont and when we again returned to Mariner Village in the fall, the cars, boys and balloons were all gone. It seemed too much like James Bond stuff, so I forgot about it and got back to our normal quiet existence. As I thought back to this incident, perhaps it would have been a perfect time to put Princes' drug sniffing prowess to work and it would really have been exciting!

Now that our potential crime scene was history, I decided that since my wife had fallen and broken many of her bones in her left foot, and was a virtual cripple for a few months, perhaps I could cheer her up a little. We, and the children have always used a little secret code when sending messages to each other that involves the numbers one, four and three. This was short for the words "I love you" that is used by far more folks that I knew about.

When the tide goes out in our area of the gulf, it is possible to walk at least one half mile out to the West on top of the squishy wet sand. Later in the day the water will return and will be three to four feet deep and be navigable by most small boats.

I mushed my way from the mangrove lined shore out about 30 yards from the shore where my feet were sinking in the sand about six inches. I proceeded to make the 1-4-3 code with letters that were about fifteen feet long in the moist sand. Even when the tides came in and out the three large numbers remained visible for about ten days. Gwen could then see them from the third floor porch, and she was thrilled. Sometimes the simplest things mean the most!

Our condominium was one of 4 four-story buildings that are situated in a gated area that is right on the edge of the gulf. Two of the buildings face the gulf and two are located closer to the wild-life protected area of marsh land that are about 100 yards from the gulf. The entire marsh is filled with every kind of bird that lives in Florida, and has a network of little canals running through it. The little mini rivers wind in and about throughout the marsh that covers about 6-10 acres. My boat was too big to navigate these waters, but I was determined to investigate with a smaller vessel. I had a close friend Don and his wife Joyce Josephic who lived on one of the canals that exited off of the gulf, and he had a small aluminum boat with a 10 horsepower outboard motor. His house was only one half mile away, and he was nice enough to let me use his craft to investigate the sanctuary.

Prince and I jumped into our car and drove to Don's to start our adventure. He was not at home, but the boat and motor were ready to go behind his house at his small dock. We climbed into the small boat and started up the outboard engine. All went well as we weaved in and out of the house-lined Canal that led us to the open water. I waved to Gwen, who was on the third floor porch as we putt putted our way towards the area behind the condos.

As we maneuvered the small canals in water that was from one to two feet deep, Prince watched the wild birds as we passed them in close proximity. I had to row the boat since the water was too shallow for the motor. After a thirty-minute paddle we reached the gulf and attempted to start the motor in order to cruise back to Don's house that was about a mile away.

The usually dependable motor refused to make any sounds, so after checking on the gas supply, I decided to row-row-row my boat back to our condo that was not too far distant. I was too tired to mess with it and decided to return it the next morning.

Early morning found Prince and I back in the small boat that still would not make any engine sounds despite a few well placed-kicks. Since I enjoy exercise, I grabbed the oars and took off with Prince as my lookout. An hour later I had rowed the boat back to Don's dock and we both jumped out onto the dock. Since no one was at home, I took the engine off and decided to pull the boat up onto the wooden dock that was about four feet above water level.

Since the small boat was not really heavy, and I had already removed the motor, it seemed like it would not be too difficult to pull the thing up onto the dock to dry. I reached down and started to pull the boat up the 4-foot incline. Just about the time that I had it out of the water, the lower end started to take on water. Now it was me against the aluminum flotation device. This stupid clunker isn't going to beat me! Much to my surprise the water flowing in was much heavier than I had expected, and it did not take long before my grip on the forward end was weakening and I was losing the battle of the canal.

When enough water had filled the lower end, I was forced to release my hold, and the boat sank back into the water, only this time it was one third full of the "aqua" that it had just previously been sitting at top of. Prince of course, had no idea of what my predicament was and he just looked at me wondering what I was going to do next. I found an old coffee can that was perfect for bailing the boat out, and I was not giving up yet! Thirty minutes later the boat was dried out, so I decided to rotate it around and pull it up bow first. I lifted it up onto the dock and started to tip the craft upwards in order to land it on top of the dock. I almost had it steep enough to raise it from the water when the stern began to fill with water exactly as the other end had done, and I struggled again only to lose another skirmish. The boat settled back down into the water and was one third full again. This was really trying my patience! This time Prince plopped himself on the deck to watch me while trying to figure out what the words were that he heard me uttering.

Well, that was it for me and my helpful attitude, so I bailed out the ark for the second and last time. Thirty minutes later, I tied the now dried out hunk of aluminum to the nearest piling and decided it would be safe there until Don came home. I picked up the outboard and with Prince bouncing along behind me headed for the side door of the garage where I found the entrance unlocked. I then opened the door and started to place the motor on the garage floor, when all hell broke loose and sirens started shrieking at me from two sides. I never knew that he had a very active and loud burglar alarm system. Of course, no one was home so Prince and I did the 50-yard dash to my car, climbed in and sped off with no signs of police or armed guards while the bells clanged on.

When I arrived home, I felt so guilty that I picked up the phone to call Don and left him a message. "Do not worry, your alarm went off because of me and not an intruder!" Unfortunately, he had already left his business an hour away to rush home after the police called him and was on his way there as I sat at home. The entire episode was over in less than two hours and would have made a very entertaining TV Blooper snippet. Don accepted my deepest apologies, and he never did hold it against Prince or I. Over the years both families have had many a chuckle as we reminisced about the adventure.

A month later one of our neighbors called me on the telephone to ask me if my small boat was still available to use on the water, because she thought that she saw a dolphin that seemed to be in some kind of trouble. Prince and I ran down to the boat that was anchored just outside of the condominium, and I realized that the object that she felt was a dolphin was not moving, and was only one hundred yards away. Prince and I waded out into the knee-deep water until we were able to reach the side of the apparently dead creature. It was about ten feet long and looked to be very heavy. It was a mature dolphin that appeared to have no marks of injury on its body, so that it must have died of old age. Dolphins in this area are frequently injured by the propeller blades of fishing boats that pass by, and in some cases they are injured by fishermen who feel like they are losing their catch to the these beautiful animals.

I made a call to the Fl. Marine Patrol and in less than an hour 4 men arrived, and with the aid of a large canvas stretcher were able to get the body into their truck. Just before they left, my Dental instincts took over and I could not resist opening the dead mammals' mouth to see what the condition of its' teeth was. I was nearly knocked over by the terrible aroma that emanated from the oral cavity that made a human's halitosis seem like a breath of fresh air. I am sure that my pal Dr. Jim had been exposed to smells equally as gross in his years of practice! Prince did not even come close, as he probably picked up this scent about the same time as we entered the water 110 yards away!

Prince adapted to condo living easily, but he had to learn to live with some restrictions involving his ability to run about unleashed, because Florida does have somewhat unfriendly reptiles such as snakes and alligators, and great caution must be exercised, particularly by animals such as retrievers who think that it is their duty and purpose in life to sniff every square inch of the land that they are presently occupying. He had never shown any inclination to attack raccoons, skunks, and porcupines in Vermont, which are always a no win situation. Nonetheless, as if to prove his manliness, he decided to exhibit an excess of interest in a nasty critter known as an opossum while taking an unleashed walk with me. As he grew close to the snarling animal with the decidedly unfriendly looking teeth, I grabbed his collar and prevented a painful bite. I believe that there was a funny character in the comics known as "Pogo," who only exhibited the better qualities of possums, as the real ones rarely react with any humorous intent.

It is really safer to chase those silly looking creatures known as armadillos, because they are not very aggressive, and sometimes appear almost stupid, and are not that much fun. As we were learning how to live in Florida, John our oldest son residing in Alexandria, Virginia was about to contribute a new chapter for my 50 Golden Years by acquiring a wonderful used and abused retriever. John and his wife had close friends who lived nearby and also owned two Goldens. This couple had reported that there was a rather run down dog that kept coming to their home, and did not seem to have any sign of an owner. Since the new dog kept returning, they began to feed him a little bit, and as he stayed close they could see that he appeared gaunt and exhibited many signs of trauma on his tangled fur covered body.

As time went on, the poor stranger seemed to consider this as his new abode, and did appear friendly. The concerned couple asked John if he might like to take this poor puppy home, and investigate his background. After two weeks of contacts with local police, and veterinarians' offices, along with the placement of newspaper ads and posters, it was determined that no one really wanted this sad looking animal. So John and his wife Cheryl took charge of the situation and with many visits to the veterinarian soon had this very dark red-coated canine looking very respectable. It is hard to imagine how anyone could mistreat an animal such as this when you looked at his beautiful face and big brown eyes. However, we know that some people treat their children in the same fashion!

He was named "Tyler" since "Velcro" had already been taken, and soon became an integral part of John's family. During our summer trip back to Vermont, we always stopped in Virginia for a few days, so that Prince could meet and bond with his new cousin Tyler and would continue this relationship when he vacationed in Vermont during the summer. Although we did not see Tyler as often as we would have liked, he became another chapter albeit a short one, in the 50 Golden Years.

Because he lived in the city, this dog's life was decidedly different from the one that Prince enjoyed in Vermont where there were few if any restrictions, and a dog could go for years without lifting a leg on the same tree. Tyler's big moments came when his Mom or Dad came home from work and took him for a walk down along the Potomac River that was only two hundred yards away. There was a nice park there that offered a good variety of droppings to sniff out. He had a very quiet demeanor, and did enjoy greeting a stranger with a wag of his tail, but some folks shied away from his friendly attempt to meet them. The biggest difference in the city was that many of the inhabitants are somewhat defensive, when it comes to greetings by strange dogs. Every one does not know what a Golden Retriever represents in the way of a loving nature, and gentle disposition, and that is their loss.

After several years of this quiet life style, that never allowed Tyler to participate in the interaction that occurs with the deer, turkeys, raccoons, porcupines, and pheasant, he with his human family moved to a house that had two acres of land, outside of Washington DC. Tyler had been through a very difficult early life, and now he was enjoying his version of 'Doggy Heaven.' in that he had a home with loving masters, a warm comfortable place to sleep, plenty of food, and now he also had some property to roam. What else is there?? His very dark silky coat had long since healed, and he spent the rest of his life as a wonderful handsome example of a good family treasure.

Now that Tyler was beginning to show his age, with an ever whitening broad face, and no longer able to move with the ease that he once enjoyed, it was time for John to think about adding another "Nugget" to the Golden family tree. This task was accomplished when John and Cheryl found a kennel that was run by a veterinarian in Ohio, and it took only a few minutes for the decision to be made to take the husky light beige colored ball of fluff with a black nose and incredibly large black eyes. Nearly every one loves a Golden puppy, a fact proven by the extensive use of them on TV commercials and catalogs of all sorts and they are seen everywhere.

Unfortunately, as the new pup named Parker started to mature and grow larger and stronger, his newly discovered mentor was showing signs of aging, even though he was only 11 years old. Although some Goldens have conditions that limit their life expectancy, our experience shows that our dogs normally live from 10-12 years, with one living to 14. Larger dogs seem to die younger than the multitude of smaller breeds, as I have seen what I call "Yappers," live to torment their owners and neighbors for 18-20 years.

Tyler followed the same pattern as he died of heart failure at age 11, and we will never know how his early maltreatment contributed to his early demise. At least he didn't suffer from any pain that we were aware of. Parker was now the man of this house and it did not take long for him to take over the reins from his predecessor. He quickly took charge of the hard rubber indestructible bones, squeaky toys, and many other "chewies" that he had inherited along with a large padded dog bed upon which Tyler had enjoyed many a restful snooze. As Parker grew into a large male with a handsome squarish head, it was discovered that his rear legs were not really performing as well as should be expected. As many know, Golden Retrievers seem to have a predisposition to have dysplastic hips, and it was time for Parker to have a complete check up with an X-ray exam of his hind quarters.

Although he was still a young dog at two years, this medical problem would have a large effect on his future life. When the radiograph was viewed, the diagnosis was confirmed. Parker had hip dysplasia affecting the right rear leg. Wanting to have the best treatment for their baby, it was decided to take him to the Veterinary Clinic and hospital at Ohio State University, where he was successfully treated and returned home with a fully functioning, but shaved right leg. I had suggested to John that he return the puppy to the Vet who had sold him for a considerable amount of money, but John and Cheryl had already fallen completely in love with this creation of God, and he is still alive today!

At the same time, another arrival, this time a two legged one that cried rather than barking, came onto the scene in the form of a healthy baby boy to be known as "JC," short for John Charles. There did not seem to be a good reason for a hip dysplasia screening for this little puppy, so he was accepted with open arms. Now Parker had a new squeaky toy to play with and all who have Goldens know how wonderfully well that this breed takes care of small critters either human or canine. This one was even better for Parker because it was also self-propelled!

As a part of our regular migration from Vermont in the summer to Florida for the winter, it was very convenient for us to stop roughly one half of the total distance which landed us in Virginia, where two of our sons lived, separated by a mere one mile. It was during these intervals that Prince and Parker would renew their friendships as long-range cousins. Prince would provide a real stress test for Parkys' legs, and both could play with J.C. Parker in particular, was a real water buff and proceeded to dive into the swimming pool at every opportunity, while Prince needed a great deal of prodding to get him immersed, and he could hardly wait to get out of the water once he was in!

Parker

While Parker remained in Virginia, Prince and his human family caromed back and forth twice a year from Florida to Vermont, the distance of approximately 1500 miles. Prince, as well as all of our Goldens was a wonderful traveling partner who never showed any signs of impatience, and was happy to relieve himself whenever we were ready. He loved to sit in the passenger seat, and lay his head on my upper thigh as I drove and could maintain this position for hours. Another example of the "Velcro Phenomenon." The travel plan sometimes included a stopover in Hilton Head, S.C. to visit friends, and he was always accepted as a cordial visitor that required no specific extra treatment. He never barked and was content to sleep on his dog bed no matter what size his room was, although he preferred to be next to our bed, it was not an absolute necessity for him. However he was happy that he had been placed between the door and us, making it impossible for us to sneak out without him! The Breckinridges were perfect hosts!

Sometimes we had to stay in motels overnight on the trips, and although some of them did not really encourage any animals, and even charged a fee for them, he was able to go unnoticed at almost every stop. When we arrived at the home of Parker, we found out that his ill-fated leg was not doing well, and that he would return to the Veterinary School for a redo of his hip surgery. The surgery again restored his ability to race about, but it had increased the total cost of his makeovers to a total of 4500 dollars, with none of the insurance coverage that is now available. Parker, despite his ability to mess up the canine medical budget, was still actually a wonderful example of a "Goofy Dog," as his demeanor proved on innumerable occasions. He was constantly trying to chase any object that could be thrown, and on too many occasions raced to the pool and leaped in just before we were ready to take him in the car, or about to entertain friends. When reprimanded, he would just give us that the goofy look as his large black eyes glistened and his soggy tail wagged like a windshield wiper, throwing off water onto anyone in the immediate vicinity.

Two years later, about the time that Parker should have been on Medicare, because he still didn't have medical insurance, he fell through the crusty snow and ice in the backyard and his "Bionic gold plated" leg found itself in a location that made it look as if it could travel in several directions at once. Talk about goofy, however even though in severe pain he maintained his usual calm demeanor, and even wagged his tail, which was happily still attached.

My son John fortunately was home at the time, and was able to load clueless Parker, who really didn't know what had happened, into the back of his four wheel drive vehicle to start the perilous journey through 4-6 inches of snow to the local Veterinarian. It would have been much easier for all involved had this happened in Vermont with Dr. Jim at the controls, but at any rate, after a consultation, John and Parker loaded back into the Explorer and drove 20 miles to the nearest animal hospital that could handle this situation. When he was carried into the clinic, it was a two-hour wait as the dog was X-rayed and checked over. The diagnosis was not a good one because Parker had fractured the leg an inch or so below the existing titanium prosthesis, and there was not enough bone left to attempt a third repair. There would be no other solution, so he remained in the clinic as John drove again 20 miles in the snow back home. Deep snow in Vermont is 20-30 inches, while in Virginia, 2-4 inches receives the same designation. The decision was to remove the leg since Parker was still a healthy strong specimen, and only eight years old. So the ex-bionic dog was now known as "The tripod", and would begin the first of many years of exhibiting, with great courage, how well he could perform activities almost as well as ever with his loveable carefree manner.

Meanwhile back at the ranch, we went back into our routine of enjoying golf and celebrating life with our other retired contemporaries. Prince had never really been very adept at hunting down golf balls, like some dogs on our golf course property. I usually let him accompany me while I pursued my greatest avocation, which is retrieving lost golf balls on the four beautiful golf courses that surrounded our condo in Innisbrook. He would patiently sit on the bank of every pond while I searched the edges looking for hidden gems with numbers and names printed on them, and tried to avoid the occasional Water Moccasin and alligators that normally lived in the lakes and swamps.

I had started searching the swamps and ponds at Innisbrook in 1979, when we first started to vacation there in the winter. I believe that I hold the undisputed record for retrieved balls at the resort. In one three-hour period, with the aid of my rubber hip boots, I was able to find 360, mostly undamaged, but muddy balls from their swampy second home. You can almost hear the sighs of relief from the balls as I plucked them from the cold, dirty water of the swamp, and cleaned them up at home in a warm bucket of soapy water spiked with small amounts of Windex and Chlorox. At first I wondered if that ball washing combination was going to create an explosion, but was soon mollified as each ball came out of the bath with the original shine and luster that rivaled any of its contemporaries sold in the pro shop for 3-4 dollars each. My friends would love me, as I would deliver a dozen or two of the resurrected spheres to them in lieu of the usual bottle of wine taken to a friendly dinner host or hostess.

This record was second only to the two man record, held by me and my middle son Brad, who had inherited the same love for helping save lonely lost 'Titleists' etc. One New year's Day, early morning at 6:30 a.m. when he was home for Christmas from the University of Vermont, Brad donned my hip boots, while I took only my knee high rubber shoes, and with our 20 foot expandable ball retrievers, went into the depths of the Florida cypress swamps. This turned out to be one of the few times that I encountered any snakes, since they are very good at moving away before you will arrive, as they sense your presence through the ground vibrations, especially if you intentionally hit the tree trunks with your metal retriever. As he entered one side of a thick swampy area about 20-30 yards across, and I entered the opposite side, the snakes therein would become confused and move away from whichever of us was closer, and in trying to avoid one of us only move into the area of the other.

Normally, very few of the "Creatures without shoulders", as one of my ball retrieving friends used to call them, are encountered and all you have to do is be patient and vigilant. As a general rule, I would prefer to spend three hours in a fruitful ball hunt than to frustrate myself for 4-5 hours playing the game that is the reason that I am finding balls. Fortunately, not too many folks like to go where I go in the woods and swamps, because if we were all in there at the same time, we would all be seeing a lot of snakes. In three hours Brad and I found collectively 425 golf balls, a record that I am sure will never be surpassed. As if to provide another reason for enjoying the sloppy excursions, I have found, over 21 years of ball chasing, other objects ranging from full cans of beer, several golf clubs that were thrown in anger, and two wrist watches, none of which were never claimed at the pro shop.

One other item that I found that was also never claimed was discovered as I crawled on hands and knees through some almost impenetrable vines and trees. As I entered a small clearing that I had passed through over the years, many times, I observed something that I had never seen before, right in my path was a large plastic bucket about 18 inches high and 18 inches wide, filled with dirt, and in the middle of it sat a stake supporting a marijuana plant that stood a healthy three feet into the air. At first I considered just ripping it out, but then I considered that one of the not too highly paid ground crew workers had planted it only 20 yards from the fairway, as a source of recreational pleasure. If there had been ten or 12 such plants, I would have reported it to the greenskeeper, but this seemed to be almost innocent. Anyway, who knows that the greenskeeper himself hadn't planted it thinking that no one in his right mind would be wandering around in that "Gator Lair"? In the years since I first visited that area, I noticed that the pot is still there, and a very large normal weed had grown through the bottom of the plastic and had anchored the old container to the ground. Who said that ball hunting isn't fun??

A few months later I was playing golf with some of my regular buddies, when a young golf pro drove up to our group and summoned me over to tell me that there was a phone call at the pro shop for me from my wife. This was before today's cell phones, so I asked my friends if they would excuse me and forget that I'd probably owed them a couple of bucks, but I needed to leave. At the pro shop I returned my wife's call, and could tell by her voice that something was wrong. It only took me about fifteen minutes to arrive at our condo, and as I entered the front door, I could see her on the kitchen floor leaning over the Golden body on the floor that was in some distress. "Honey," she said, "I think Prince is having a heart attack." I quickly knelt down and put my ear to his chest, and looked into his lovely brown eyes, and I knew immediately he had only a thread of life left, and he had held on until his Dad could hold him for just one more time. In seconds he was gone as Gwen and I both hugged each other with him in the middle, and said together "I love you Prince". Now another of my beloved Goldens had joined his predecessors in what we consider "Doggy Heaven", hopefully to be revisited.

Of course, it is never easy to see one of your beloved Goldens leave this life, but at least it was a painless and quick way for him to depart. I placed my hand over his mouth and nose, to try to detect any sign of life, and there was none, he was gone. We were in Florida, and Dr. Jim was not available, so I called our local Vet and told him what had happened, and he asked me to bring him right over. I picked up his lifeless body that still had it's Golden silky coat, and proceeded down the rear stairs of the condo to place him into the back of the station wagon, the same one that he had happily jumped into the day before.

When I arrived at the Veterinary office, he met me and expressed his condolences, since he also knew Prince from previous visits and understood how much I loved him. One of his assistants lifted Prince from the car, and took him into the building and that ended another beautiful chapter of my 50 Golden years. It was then that I realized again how fragile our lives and the lives of our beloved pets really are, and that we must enjoy them to the fullest each day, while realizing that they are only given to us on a temporary basis. If only all of us would understand that simple basic truth, perhaps we would live out our lives in a more meaningful way.

It took a while to realize that Prince would no longer be a part of our lives, and that a new condominium regulation that restricted dogs over 22 pounds from living on property, might prevent us from replacing him. This idea was extremely disturbing and hard to fathom, especially since the floor that we lived on had four or five small dogs whose constant yapping and whining made us realize what a prize we had enjoyed with our 80 pound, non-barking dog. As we began to pack up for the trip back to Vermont for the summer, we pondered about the fact that maybe this was our last big dog, and that we could just enjoy the dogs that our children had. After all, two of them were Goldens and one was a yellow lab, and he was after all in the same overall category of "Retrievers."

CHAPTER 15

Northward Bound

There was a different feeling, as we proceeded to return to Vermont. We were so used to having a large Golden presence, using a fair amount of space in the back of the car and now it seemed unusually empty. It wasn't really, as we always seemed to look quite like the characters in the old television show "Jed Clampett," that had stuff packed in everywhere. There were clothes, food, furniture, computers, and two golf bags, and I thought about where another dog would possibly fit, but I knew we could make room for it if we had to.

When we arrived in Virginia, and drove up to John's home, we were, as always, welcomed by the tail wagging, joyful greeting extended to us by "The Tripod." He had no way of knowing that there would not be another reunion with his pal Prince, and he did seem to look confused when only two human forms emerged from the car. After he exhibited how well he could run on his three legs, he settled down to receive his share of petting and stroking. That would never change, and he knew it. It seems that Goldens just know that they were put on Earth to love and be loved, so why change?

We normally did not stay more than a few days with the families of the two boys in Virginia, as Gwen tried to live by her father's favorite pronouncement that "Fish and company stink in three days." I think that is the way he stated that, and he was usually correct. We were only back in the Quechee house a few weeks, when the thoughts about puppies began to be brought up in our normal conversations. It didn't take much longer for me to go to the computer, and its dreaded Internet, and peruse the network for locations that might lead to the discovery of "Oh no not another puppy." Since we were both thinking about the same thing, and we represented a quorum, the search committee of two was formed to see if there was more Gold in our future. By chance, we came upon an ad for puppies in a northern town of Vermont near the Canadian border, which was only about 60 miles north of our house.

The town was Newport, and it happened to be where a dentist friend of mine practiced. When I was able to reach him by phone, he was happy to tell me that the kennel with the available pups was one of good repute and would bear further investigation. The next call was to the kennel itself to find out if we were too late to prospect for more Gold? The woman affirmed that there were two puppies left, and that we could visit them tomorrow. The drive was not long, and was shortened by a mind-boggling feeling that we might again be the proud parents of another Golden. Each one of our previous Goldens had brought so much pleasure and love, that it was not going to be possible for us to be a complete family without another one. It is not a coincidence that this breed is used to bring joy to a countless number of retirement homes, rehabilitation centers, and even hospital children's wards.

Northern Vermont towns are mostly small in size, and each one has its own particular charm. When we were finally able to find the modest house on a back road, we were like kids anticipating a big event, and in actuality it was to be exactly that. The young woman who answered the door invited us into her living room, and then went into another room to "Release the hounds." Two little puppies raced into the room, each one falling over the other to see which one would reach us first. It was over in a minute, and the decision would be easy in the end, but which one would we like? The male was a darker shade of red that resembled his father and the female was lighter, as her mother's genes would dictate. The breeder really wanted to keep the female in order to be able to make more puppies, but we were now so unsure of our choice, that we offered to take both of them and keep them together. She reluctantly agreed, and so we had a deal, and one that we never regretted, as I will relate in upcoming chapters.

The car had already been partially set up as a sort of compartment with blankets and a barrier to keep them in the rear section of the mobile kennel. Off we went with some small amounts of chirping and other sounds that puppies make before they really learn to bark. Actually we thought that most of it always came from the male, because as it turned out the little blond female didn't utter a bark but once in her entire life, and that was when she was six years old. When we were about halfway home, Gwen and I almost simultaneously remarked, "Oh my, I think that someone has had an accident," as the distinctive odor of puppy excrement began to permeate the small interior of the vehicle. Oh well, they are after all little guys, and this is a natural thing to do. For all we knew this was probably the first time that these little charmers had ever been riding in an automobile. I stopped the car in order to clean up the small accident, as the pups wagged their little stubby tails and looked about as innocent as possible, neither one admitting to the act. Once the odor associated with natures' call had left the area, we were happy to hug the puppies and get a chance to enjoy their real puppy scent, which is really very nice.

Prince & Angel
Too 1996

Prince Too
1996

Gwen—Prince Too

Angel—Prince Too
1996

Angel—Prince Too—Jack 1997

Angel—Prince Too—Jack
1997

Angel—Prince Too
1997

When we completed the drive home, I went to my wood pile in order to find the pieces of wood that I would need to make a temporary area that would keep the babies in the outside air, while still making sure that they could not escape. On the lower level of our split-level home, there was a room that I used as an office that had a sliding door exiting onto a small 8 ft.by 12 ft. deck. This would be their home for a few months and I added a small, hinged door that gave access to the large backyard and surrounding wooded area. We had never had two small puppies at the same time except when Missy delivered her 9 puppies twenty years earlier. I had forgotten just how important it was for them to have close contact with each other, especially as they slept, usually with the male dog resting his head on his sister's back.

Now it was time to choose names for the couple, since no one uses their complicated A.K.C. registered names, and these guys would not even be used for breeding. Since Prince One had always been such a superb companion and family member, it seem to be a nice way to honor his memory by naming him, not Prince II, or Prince Two or even Prince Also, but Prince Too. Since our little female had such a quiet demeanor, and a sweet face, she would be named Angel, and in order to relate better with Prince she became Angel Princess. A name that as time went by could not have been better chosen, as she was to grow up living up to her name. Dr. Jim was able to perform all of the necessary shots and associated details. These jobs would be some of the last ones that Jim would ever do, as he had a severe stroke that left him partially paralyzed and unable to work from then on. However, he had just hired a new young couple that were both Veterinarians, who would continue his practice as well as taking good care of our twins.

Jim had to spend some time in rehabilitation, and because of his strong will and stubborn nature, seemed to be able to work his way back slowly. I was able to get him out of the house to attend the weekly Rotary Club meetings that we both enjoyed. Jim had been a great Rotarian for over forty years and I was a member for thirty years. It is a great organization world-wide, and we would meet every Wednesday at noon, after which in the summer he and I would resume our battle for the "Hoof and Mouth" Trophy, and in the winter we played a game called "platform tennis" with our usual golf buddies as our opponents. Platform or paddle tennis was played on a miniature tennis court that was raised off the ground about 3-4 ft. and was completely encircled by a tight chicken wire fence that extended 12-15 feet upwards. The court lines and the net were comparable to tennis, and the major difference was, that the ball was hit by a perforated wooden paddle that was about twice the size of a ping-pong paddle. The ball could be played off of the fencing before it hit the ground. If you were not up to skiing or ice-skating, this was a wonderful way to keep fit in the cold weather.

For the first years after his stroke, I managed to coax Jim in his wheelchair, to attend these meetings and for a 30 minute period following, he would at least try to chip or putt on the putting green that was part of the Woodstock Country Club. It was very difficult for Jim to accept his physical impairment, because he had practiced summer and winter, often in very difficult circumstances, with very small and very large animals. The farmers loved him since he was never too busy to tend to their needs, night or day, and all with a fee that was affordable. Small animal owners were served with the same care, and I often wondered how anyone could be able to treat such a large variety of patients. At least for me, teeth were all the same, regardless of the type of person that they were attached to. I did however, once remove a tooth from a deer that had been shot by a friend, because I was interested to see how similar they might be to the human tooth. I found that you could estimate the age of the deer by observing the amount of wear on the teeth, where in the case of most humans, it is far more reliable to ask them to reveal the answer to the age question.

As the twins both kept growing into beautiful full-grown adults, Dr. Jim's condition grew slowly worse and he kept slowing down in his efforts to get out onto the putting green, and in addition, he started to lose interest in almost everything. Even Dorothy, his devoted wife, could not seem to get him to participate in any activity that he had in earlier years thoroughly enjoyed. Every one handles the physical problems in a different manner, but I know that if the situation had been reversed, Jim would have badgered me (as only Jim could do!) However, even though we had been great friends for thirty years, I just could not get myself to push him beyond what I really thought he was capable of.

Over the next year he regressed to the point where he was in bed about 80 percent of the time, and did not seem to even want to listen to the radio. Sadly his mind seemed to be clear and he was cognizant of everything, but he just gave up. Our "Hoof and Mouth" trophy would never again be contested, and even though I had been lucky enough to win it over the last few years and I wanted him to keep it by his bed, so that he could reflect back on the wonderful memories that it represented. It remained settled with him until the frail body gave out and his heart ceased to function, ending his journey in 1997. The Trophy sits proudly on my desk to this day, and people often ask what it was for, but no words could explain what this partially tarnished silver golf trophy really meant to a small, devoted group of Vermont golf addicts.

Now a new era would begin with our two latest editions that now would be watched over by the equally new young Veterinarian couple Drs. Brad and Angela Burrington. When we made our annual return to Florida this time, we would be returning to our first stand-alone home which had required only a move of just five miles from the waterfront, storm battered, condo that served us well for over ten years. The friendships that we had made there are still very solid to this day, and we visit there frequently. Our new house was a single story home with a nice pond in the backyard that separated the one-acre of land from the large lake behind it known as Lake Tarpon, a beautiful boating and fishing Mecca. One of the first things to make us realize that we did indeed live in Florida was to discover the resident 6-foot alligator that was subsequently named "Chomp" by the majority vote of the grandchildren. Our new home was only a mile as the crow flies directly over the large lake from the golf course at Innisbrook. However, it was a drive of 6-7 miles away if your boat was stored and a car was used to reach our golf destination.

The new home had an enclosed pool area, which was soon to change the life of one of our new twin puppies. Even though Gwen and I thoroughly enjoyed having a pool, I in particular, had to be extremely concerned about excess sun exposure, since I had already had one melanoma on my back and had lost three friends from this very misunderstood form of skin cancer. If you are a person who has had a significant amount of sun exposure due to outdoor activities associated with work or pleasure, you must have a better understanding of how serious the melanoma form of skin cancer can be. I will talk more about this in later chapters.

Neither of the twins would voluntarily enter the lake or a pool or the ocean at any time, and this fact is a little unusual for all of the Retriever breeds. When the puppies were less than a year old, I had offered to clear some nuisance trees from the perimeter of my neighbors home, and she promised to bake me a nice cake as repayment. Later that day, my friend was in the process of fulfilling that promise, and was delivering the tasty morsel to us by way of the back entrance to the pool enclosure. As she carried the prize alongside the edge of the pool, she attracted the attention of the two little ones, since this was a new and very interesting olfactory stimulus. As Angel hurried over to the object that was being conveyed along the pool edge, she did not pay enough attention to the proximity of the water, and when she tried to get a close up smell she disappeared into the water and immediately sank to the bottom of the 5 foot shallow area. It didn't seem shallow to her, since she had never been under water in her life before, and this experience would result in her abject fear of H2O in any form.

It was even difficult for her to sit in our shower and have a bath without a panic attack for the remainder of her life. Although our friend quickly reached down to retrieve her, but the damage was done. From that day on when anyone entered the pool she would hide behind any object that was available, and stay cuddled up against the stucco wall, sometimes trembling and definitely looking for some sympathy and hoping for a big hug. "Do anything but just don't drag me into that stuff!" she would plead. Prince would stay over near her as if to help protect her from the dreaded wet liquid, but he really didn't want to go in there either, although once he was in, he rather enjoyed it.

As the two dogs began to grow into beautiful adults, I would take them with me on walks without leases down to the large lake that was only one hundred yards behind our own little gator pond. Even though both of them loved to sniff every square inch of the ground, they would venture only to the edge of the pond, and were never in danger of an alligator encounter. At the end of the paved road that went past our house down to the real large lake, there was a boat ramp where I could dump my little 12 ft. boat into the lake. There was a nice deck area, which split up into 12-14 individual boats slips that were only used by the residents of our small area of homes. This area of decking was about 150 feet long, and was also used for bass fishing.

The area surrounding this portion of the lake was fairly heavily wooded with moss covered cypress trees, and large pine trees surrounded by various sharp pointed members of the palm tree family. There were of, course, some very large gators in this lake, and always drew attention from boaters that passed by but they really didn't cause much harm as they tried to stay away from any human beings. Most problems stemmed from the fact that some humans never realize that it is not their duty, nor is it in their best interest, to feed any wild creatures at any time. Since alligators were quite territorial, even on a golf course, they will react to anything or anyone that invades their "space", in somewhat the same way as you would react to any intruder in your home.

One of the problems that I encountered, since I had volunteered to be in charge of our "Neighborhood Watch" program, was how to prevent speeding and other breaches of safety in our area. Since we did have a large contingent of fairly affluent young people in our division, there were many activities that I as a senior citizen, did not consider as advisable or necessary. As the road past my home was used very little at night, it became a magnet for groups of teenagers with alcohol and unfortunately drugs, which are easily available. I didn't know where the parents were, but I did know where the local Sheriff's department was, and they usually responded in a timely manner to disperse the supposed "Next Generation of Leaders, Heaven help us!

On one bright Florida morning, I accompanied my two buddies down the road for their daily nature walk, which took us past the small pond and down to the boat ramp area. My somewhat timid companions did not follow me out onto the dock, as they didn't ever feel comfortable walking on a wooden surface that has spacing between the boards. I did not want them to stay alone, so I only proceeded onto the dock only 10 yards and looked around to see if any gators were near the edge. Seeing none, my eyes slowly proceeded to scan the weed-clogged area that lay between the shoreline and the boats slips. I was hoping to get a glimpse of a fish or two, but instead I noticed something under the waters' surface, that did not really belong there. It looked metallic and appeared to be several feet long. It certainly was not a normal marine object, and it did not move, so what was it? I broke a large branch from a nearby tree, and tried to move the thing but it was too heavy to budge, however I could now get a closer look at it as the weeds were parted. It appeared to be a cylinder of some sort, but what was it doing here? It looked to be either green or blue, but the weed cover made it impossible to be sure. Since as a dentist, I was used to seeing containers like this in hospital and dental offices, I thought that they were either Oxygen or Nitrogen Oxide, depending on the actual color of the cylinder. Either way they did not belong here, so I decided to call in my friends from the Sheriff's Department.

A van with several officers arrived within an hour, and they were equipped with a small boat, and two men had wetsuits along with their scuba gear. It was beginning to look like a James Bond movie in a most unlikely setting. As my two make believe police dogs and I observed from the weathered planks, one of the two divers that were now in chest deep water, pulled a large blue tank from the dark lake and dragged it on to the beach. I could see by its color that it was a navy blue Nitrogen Oxide or "Laughing gas" cylinder and that it was far from its normal home. I had used a nitrogen oxide set up in my practice as it had many good applications. Many patients loved it as it simulated a "high" that resembled the one achieved by 2-3 highballs. I used it when some patients, who were so frightened by the thought of an injection of Novocaine, needed it to get them through their wimpy ability to cope. It was only when a teenager told me after her appointment, that she loved the "Laughing Gas" because it gave her the same feeling that she got from using marijuana. Having no actual practice in the use of such junk, I decided that no one in my office would ever get the simulated high again, so a week later, I sold all of my N2O equipment, including blue tanks, to an oral surgeon in the next town.

Now here many years later, I was witnessing the recovery of the very same blue tanks, only why would they be at the bottom of my lake? We all were awestruck as the two frogmen moved around in the dark water and were finding more containers. In less than thirty minutes they had stacked up 9 blue tanks that were all empty. Even when devoid of the "funny gas," they were too heavy to float, but nine of them in the same location were a real mystery. One or two of the tanks had some controls still attached to the tops, but all were used up. It would not have been unusual for a delivery truck that served a hospital or a large dental clinic to have that large amount of cylinders, but there would be no reason to find that cache at the bottom of the lake out in the country. As the divers were completing their thorough scan of the area, two other officers were lowering them into a truck. The sheriff who appeared to be in charge, thanked me for the call and assured me that I would get a call in a day or so with some information.

True to his word, 48 hours later, I received his call and was told that each of the large tanks had been stolen from individual dental offices and medical clinics around the county over a period of two years. The assumption was that kids either in small gangs or as pairs had been breaking into offices and even delivery trucks, to steal the potentially dangerous canisters. Laughing gas, or N2O can be fatal if taken in large doses. The conclusion to be drawn by the police was that the stupid, but clever kids were using the "Giggly Gas" to get high, either there at my lake at night, or another clandestine location nearby. They would then simply dump the tanks off of my dock, where they thought that they would not be found. I never did find out if the authorities ever did find the culprits, but the whole incident made my wife and I wonder what the hell is wrong with these kids today.

Later that week, I contacted a fence company and together with them, set up a date to install posts with a pad locked chain stretched across the road. I locked this chain at 8 p.m. every night, so that no cars would be able to deliver its load of brain dead juveniles, whose parents were clueless, down to this beautiful park again!

When the stream of weekend visitors going past my house had stopped, it was time to try to return to the normal life that I had expected in Florida. The small pond beyond the house did have "Chomp," and he or she whichever it was, cruised across the smooth water like a small submarine several times a day. Even though I was certain that Angel and Prince were too large for the gator to attack, there were always articles in local newspapers reporting the losses of small animals, dogs and cats that were attributed to "Gator Gulps." Whenever my pups wandered near the edge of the water, which wasn't too often, and Chomp was visibly noticing them, I used an old pellet gun to bounce a few BB'S off of his back. The gator would quietly submerge and move stealthfully to a remote area of the pond, probably wondering what that was that stung him. Actually there are not many serious gator attacks in Florida, but I was not going to have my Goldens exposed to even a hint of danger.

It was nice to have a small resident gator living in my pond, but I really wanted a bunch of nice bass to make my pond an exciting place for our 11 grandchildren to fish while visiting. I enlisted the aid of an avid fisherman, Bill Crorey, who lived at our nearby golf resort, but who actually was a better angler than a golfer. The hooks on his fishing rod serve him better than the hooks that came from his golf clubs. If I could only have Bill catch a few large mouth bass in the big lake just a hundred yards away, we could transport them back to my pond and in a short time, it would resemble a fish hatchery. The kids would be in "Halibut Heaven," when they came on vacation to visit.

One day Bill arrived with his lovely wife Betty, who would keep Gwen company while the guys were hard at their fishing chores. He had all of the necessary fishing gear that included the never fail plastic worms, plus a myriad of other bait that could catch anything from a minnow to a great white shark. He had it all and in addition, he had the necessary confidence and knowledge to make this a great success. We both made a large size Manhattan cocktail, and walked to the lake with the dogs.

He had the fishing equipment and a drink, while I had a large plastic bucket to carry the catch and my drink. We strolled out to the end of the dock and I explained to him the recent police action that had just taken place right were we would fish.

In about thirty minutes we got our first bite, and as Bill promptly landed it, I filled my plastic bucket with water so that the fish would survive the trip back to my pond. It was pretty small, but I didn't complain about it, as it was a good start. It was about an hour later that our glasses were empty, and I was beginning to doubt that Bill was really the "Michigan state champion bass fisherman," when suddenly his pole bent almost in half as he exclaimed "I've got a beauty." He reeled in the "Mini Whale" of a large mouth bass, and I managed to get it into the net without losing it or my life. It was growing dark, and the mosquitoes were just coming out when we dumped the clunker into the bucket with the baby first catch. I hoped that the newcomer would not find and eat the small bass that was very much in danger, because we needed all the fish that we could catch.

It was time to go back to the house and show the girls the result of our hard work. I found that the large plastic bucket with two fish and full of water filled to the overflow point, was going to be too heavy to carry all the way back to the house, and it would be advisable to jettison some water onto the dock.

As I poured out the heavy liquid, a strange event took place when the small fish at the bottom became frightened and must have attacked the giant large-mouth, resulting in the big boy making a prodigious effort to escape the container, much like "Shamu" at Sea World. Before I could grab the slippery monster, he had jumped off the dock flooring right back into the lake from which it had just been hoisted. Bill was walking ahead of me when he heard the great splash and in the fading light said, "What the hell was that?" I replied, "I think it was a fish," as I gazed sheepishly into the now nearly empty bucket, "But I think that the little one is still there!" "You dummy, this was not supposed to be a catch and release program," We both laughed and moved towards the house to get a bigger, better drink after I dumped the remaining water and the little survivor fish into my pond. At least we have a start, even though a small one! It was a good thing that Bill had a great sense of humor. It would be a great story to relate to our friends in Vermont where we would soon return for other summer.

Angel—Prince Too 2000

Prince Too 2000

CHAPTER 16

Not All Is Fun in the Sun

Since Golden Retrievers may star in Hollywood films as soccer and basketball heroes, there have never, to my knowledge, been any that have played golf. Golf has played a large part in my life, and in the life of our family over the fifty years that are included in my 50 Golden years story as well. All four of our children and my wife play golf now and then, at least, and I could probably write a short book about our collective golf experiences. I would like to relate just a few golf moments that I think are quite novel and pretty likely once in a lifetime occurrences

One occurred about thirty years ago and involved my great "Hoof and Mouth" friend, Dr. Jim, and two of our other regular gang. We were playing the 15th hole at the Woodstock Country Club in Vermont, a course that I've played on for almost forty years. It is a par three that plays about 140-160 yards depending on the tee. On this Wednesday afternoon, the first player drove his ball out over the small river that runs in front of the green, and ended up about ten feet from the pin, and was a great shot. The next player duplicated that shot and was pretty close to the pin. Then came the indomitable Dr. Jim, who had a better swing than the normal results would indicate. He took a nice cut at the ball, and before I even had a chance to offer my usual brand of needling advice, the ball started out right at the flag stick on a great trajectory and to everyone's amazement, bounced twice and disappeared directly into the hole for an ace, his second career Hole in One.

We all did our 1980s version of a high five, as he pretended that it was not really that difficult, so what did we expect? When the celebration calmed down, it was my turn to try to drop one right on top of his, so that he could see who was really the better player! I swung with a fair amount of confidence and watched with pleasure as the ball bored its way through the air on a very good path, until forces of gravity took over and dropped the ball unceremoniously into the middle of the 20 foot wide river, never to be seen again.

After recovering from my disappointment, I dropped another ball next to the swirling brook, and chipped over the hazard onto the green, where I 2-putted for a double bogey 5. All I could think of was that I had just lost four strokes to Jim, and I wasn't paying as much attention as I should have, as my two other playing partners calmly both sunk their great birdie two putts. On the next tee, Dr. Jim coyly asked, "Jack, did you notice that your score of five was the total of all three of the other players combined?" my reply was somewhat subdued, but I managed to explain that my feat of equaling their five with my five was far more difficult to achieve that his little lucky hole in one! Of course, he did not really believe that, but it proved to be a truthful statement, when my youngest son, my daughter, and I all made holes in one on this very same hole over the next ten years following.

Golf is a great game, and nearly anything can happen. My wife, although not as avid as I, does enjoy a weekly game with friends at Innisbrook, and she has made two holes in one herself. She tells me that it is all luck when those things happen, but when I made my 8th one this year, she admitted that maybe there was some skill involved. That is one reason why we can be still happily married over 52 years. Another fun thing that only avid golfers would even notice in conversation was that I was able or lucky enough to shoot my age at 75 and 76. Previous to that, I had been able to shoot only my weight for many years before.

One of the more serious events in my life was at least in part due to the many years of sun exposure on the golf course, as well as on the beach vacations that we all enjoyed. At the end of our summer in Vermont, one of the items on my health agenda was to have a complete screening by a good friend Dr.Baughman, a dermatologist whose office I had visited in the summers for over twenty years. I had treatment for a small malignant melanoma on my back in the early 90s, however because of it's location, I could not see it myself. It is a good idea to have a friend or spouse examine your neck and back areas that are not easily visible to you. I never gave any consideration to the real problem that melanoma of any size and any location could present. A few days before we were to head south again, Gwen and I noticed an area about the size of a small finger-nail, on my right forearm. The lesion had some of the usual color characteristics of a melanoma, and just didn't look right.

Melanoma has certain basic diagnostic appearances, namely; Asymmetric shape (one half does not match the other), irregular Borders, more than one Color and the size is larger in Diameter than a pencil eraser. A top researcher at Emory Medical school in Atlanta Georgia, mentioned to me at the time that my eldest son had a diagnosis of melanoma on his neck, and that each melanoma has a life of its own, so to speak, and there are not always set patterns to search for. In any case, early detection is the key to the cure of this insidious killer. One of my sons had an employee whose wife did not survive a melanoma of her eye at the young age of 32, because of the difficulty of detection in that area. No place on the body is immune from this cancer, and you do not have to have had any sun exposure on that area. Even heredity is known to play an important part in the incidence of this dreaded cancer.

The day before we left Vermont, our dermatologist was able to see me in order to do the biopsy on my arm, which he quickly sent to the pathology lab. Our schedule called for us to leave the next day, so my doctor said he could send the biopsy results to me in Florida in a few days. I had already made an appointment at the Mayo Clinic in Jacksonville, with a plastic surgeon. Since time is of the essence with melanoma, I was very happy to receive the result of the tests, but I was not so pleased when I read the diagnosis of melanoma. The surgery was scheduled for a few days later at Mayo. The major problem with this cancer is it's ability to reach a certain depth in the various layers of the skin, and when it achieves that level, it becomes almost impossible to halt its invasive spread to other areas of the body, in particular the brain and the lungs.

As soon as we arrived back in Florida, we set sail for Jacksonville, Fl. Mayo, since that was our medical version of "Mecca." My biopsy had been forwarded from Dartmouth Medical Center in New Hampshire, and my good friend and plastic surgeon, Dr.Galen Perdikis, was ready to go. One of the fascinating areas of the procedure was a radiology procedure where a radio-active dye was injected into the area surrounding the biopsy area. It was then necessary to lie completely still for twenty minutes or so, which can seem like an eternity, while a scanning device would move slowly up my arm tracking the dye as it moved up the arm towards the lymph nodes that were in my axilla (Arm Pit). The main idea of this was to see where the dye that followed the same path as the possible spread of the melanoma would travel to. The so called "Sentinel Node" that would be the lymph node that would pick up the first invasive efforts of the cancer. If that node showed any microscopic sign of the melanoma, then we would know that a metastasizing procedure was underway, and that spelled "big trouble."

The surgery at the original site of the biopsy was performed in an area that would be wide enough to ensure that the lesion was completely removed. This area covered about eight-ten inches, and required about 40 sutures. The lymph area in the axilla is a part of our natural protection system, and would have been the first place that the cancer, or an infection would go to. This "Sentinel Node" and ten other nodes in the area were all removed, and fortunately showed no signs of cancer. This was a great relief, and the only negative was that the area still retains a certain amount of numbness. But sometimes my brain does the same thing, according to my wife, and this is not related to any surgical procedure. This successful surgery by Dr. Perdikis has been followed up by ten years of six monthly check ups that includes chest x-rays, CAT scans, and various blood tests. All of this caused by what looked like a simple, colored area on my forearm, that if it had been neglected for a few months, would have prevented this book from being written, and perhaps I would have had to return the "Hoof and Mouth" trophy to Dr. Jim in "Heaven!"

Ever since this encounter with the "Mother of all skin cancers", both Gwen and I both extol the virtues of staying away from sun exposure, and the liberal use of sun tan lotions of at least a level of 30. Another fact worth noting is that there is presumed to be a genetic component to this cancer, and this was proved out in the form of a mole on the neck of my oldest son, that exhibited a color change that was also diagnosed to be Malignant Melanoma.

While recovering from this operation, I was kept company by my buddies, Prince and Angel, as I was able to accompany them on their daily nature walks down to the lake. In some ways our Florida paradise was very much like Vermont. The wooded area of pine, oak, and cypress trees by the lake was a refuge for many white tail deer that included a nice 6-point buck. Even the Great Blue Herons and the beautiful white Egrets were found in both regions even though separated by 1200 miles. In Florida, we had Armadillos, possums, and various snakes, while our Vermont backyard yielded in this year alone, a Moose, a Mama Bear with three large cubs, a flock of wild turkeys, multiple deer families, several raccoons, and a fat porcupine. For the most part there was little to fear from our Vermont menagerie, however Florida critters are cut from a different cloth. Opossums can inflict pain and a nasty bite, gators can too, but the snakes are the ones to be most fearful of.

One day while gardening around the house, I uncovered a beautiful red, black and yellow-banded snake that did not seem to be too active, and did not glide away quickly as most snakes do. However, because of my extensive experience in golf ball hunting, I recognized it as a coral snake. It was about 14-16 inches long, however don't be fooled by its diminutive size! I decided I did not want him in any proximity to my Golden friends, so since I had a nice shovel, I was able to make it into three equal sections with two well placed strokes. My golf experience has provided me with a good measure of hand to eye coordination. I placed the three pieces, after they stopped moving, into a plastic food storage bag and delivered it to my next door neighbors back porch, so that her small son might have a great exhibit for his next day's "show and tell" at school. She was not home, so I left it at the back door, however I never received a thank you note, so I perceived that maybe she did not consider it as a good neighborly gesture. After all, I am not "Steve Irwin!" There had been an article in the local newspaper that said that a little boy had picked up a coral snake, not knowing its ability to inflict a dangerous bite, and was in a coma for a month before he recovered. They are very beautiful, but equally deadly.

The fact that these slithery creatures are often buried in the dirt, caused me great concern when my two pups were found on several occasions digging with great energy and fervor, trying to make a hole under the fence that surrounded their 10 foot by 14 foot pen, just outside of the pool enclosure. It is amazing how much dirt, or in this case sand, that two dogs could manage to relocate in a matter of a few minutes. By the looks of them at work, they even used their snouts to move the sand, as their noses were covered with white granules. In the end, I had to place chicken coop wire about four to 6 inches under the soil for a few feet around the fence lines to end their quest for freedom.

CHAPTER 17

Life Is a Beach

Since melanoma can be a life altering experience, Gwen came to me one day with a startling announcement. Although this house on the lake was by far our most favorite house ever, she completely surprised me by suggesting that we should consider a move that would take us closer to Mayo Clinic in Jacksonville, Fl. She felt that the future might hold many more medical visits to the clinic, and that we should move closer to the doctors there. I knew that this would be a great sacrifice for her, because our long-standing friendships at Innisbrook would suffer because of the four-hour ride necessary to get to the East Coast. We may also have to give up our golf membership, that we both enjoyed since 1979.

The other side of the coin however, from my point of view, was that we could still live part-time in Vermont during the summer, and if we could find a place near the Atlantic Ocean, I could fulfill my dream of living at or near the beach. I had always had a great love of the sights, sounds, and smells of the ocean, and its' marvelous beaches. We were sure that even though Prince and Angel would probably not race enthusiastically into the waves in search of any thrown object like most retrievers, they would love to walk the sandy beaches, and best of all use their sniffing ability to search out all sorts of stuff, live and dead, that lay on or under the sand. One of the great joys of the ocean shores is that with the tides every day, there was delivered to you a new fresh environment to gaze at or walk upon.

When I was a small boy in the late 30s and early 40s, my parents always took my sister Peg and I down for a summer vacation to the shores of South Jersey, at Ocean City. In those times there was train service from Philadelphia to Ocean City, and on into Atlantic City. My father rented a house for fifty dollars a month, where my Mom, sister and I would be able to stay while my father, a research chemist for Atlantic Refining Oil company, could visit us on weekends, and return to work without too much hassle. Dad was a very quiet man whose life was controlled by scientific matters and pressures, and he only lived to age 46, when he died of a heart attack.

His short vacation time was important to him, and he spent at least half of each day fishing in the surf or the beach, catching flounder, croakers and weakfish, along with an occasional sand shark and Sea Robin. I, of course, was delighted to be with him, but 60 minutes in the crashing surf was an eternity to me, while he could stand there for three or four hours and enjoy the solitude. I then had to amuse myself with a kite or dig sand castles with my sister. I even had an invention that never worked out, wherein I built a large 6 foot long kite out of pieces of thin wood and newspapers, that I attached a small pulley to, that would allow me to attach a fishing line that would drop into the water once I was able to get the kite out over the deeper part of the ocean. Of course, I forgot to figure out what would happen if a large fish came along and dragged the contraption out of the sky into the ocean, and all would be lost. Nothing ventured nothing gained!

After a short period of searching, we finally found a location that almost seemed to be too perfect to be true. We came to a small town named Palm Coast, Fl. that was equally distant from Daytona Beach on the south and St. Augustine on the north. The Florida coast is much less busy in that area along Route A1A, and that alone played a large part in our decision. The other item that sealed the deal was that the house we chose was sitting on the golf course, and was situated only three hundred yards or so from the ocean itself. We were delighted with this situation, and the dogs would soon learn that the beach there was practically uninhabited. We rarely encountered another person on our daily walks, so that they could roam the sands unleashed for a mile or more, attempting to chase the Pelicans and Sandpipers that were so plentiful.

Of course, running in the sand and rolling on top of old seaweed and an occasional dead fish did not make them perfect house-guests, but they were very happy. Even though these two were littermates, Angel had a lighter color fur with a coarser texture than Princes' darker red silkier coat. Angel also suffered from skin irritations, particularly in her ears that needed help from various types of medications. Neither dog ever had fleas, and ticks were few and far between. The new preventive medications really work! Whenever Angel had a bout with infection, Prince would lovingly lick her ears to try to clean out the "gook", but I am afraid that his attention did more harm than good.

Both dogs had wonderful, loving dispositions, and Angel would love to snuggle up to me on a couch, or even on the floor, and create the "Velcro effect." She would continue to lean into you while at the same time make small whimpering sounds that I am certain I could interpret as loving words from this very sensitive creature.

Prince, on the other hand, being a male, also enjoyed a hug, but his tendency was to pull away a little as if he wanted to be sure that he was after all a "man dog," and didn't want to be thought of as anything but that. He did, however, like to lick on your hand or arm, almost like you were his favorite bone. Prince made life a little easier around the house since he did not shed much hair, while Angel left little light-weight puff-balls of blond hair that accumulated in every corner of the porch, and could have filled a pillow. Angel however, was perhaps the sweetest Golden of my "50 Golden Years," and she had a sad look in her eyes that perhaps was a clue about her future.

Another very unusual characteristic was that she had an apparent inability to bark at any time. I had asked our vet if it was possible that she could not bark, but he didn't believe that this was the case. He was proven correct in his assessment when we were returning from our beach walk one late afternoon, and "Hunter," a neighbors' Border Collie came rushing toward her at full speed from the rear and barked in his usual friendly manner. Angel was so surprised by this mock attack, that she uttered a "woof" of her own that left us all laughing in wonderment, since we now knew that she could bark after all. She never did bark again ever, but not because she didn't have the ability to.

During the beach strolls, Gwen and I also kept an eye on the edge of the water line to see if we could find any interesting shells that might have washed up during the change of tide. There are always various types of jelly fish that the dogs fortunately had no interest in, but on rare occasions, (only two in five years), I came across an artifact known as a "Crucifix fish." This was actually the main part of the skeleton of a large catfish that looked exactly like a "Crucified Jesus," and was a beautiful example of how God and nature can work in unusual ways. When this sun-bleached skeleton is put into a shadow box frame, it adds a very unusual conversation piece for a home.

Perhaps, the most touching thing that my lover dog "Angel," used to do, was to bring back to us an object that was found frequently on the beach, but not deemed worthy of that much attention. However, when Angel walked about a quarter mile ahead of us down the coastline and then made their way back with a starfish held gently in her front teeth by the tip, which left the main body hanging down like a Christmas ornament. She would proudly plop herself at your feet and present her gift of love. We had certainly aptly named her "Angel Princess," as she had all of the qualities that an Angel would possess. Prince on the other hand, was more likely to find a half eaten fish carcass, and then proceed to roll over onto his back on top of this smelly carcass and wriggle the ex-fish and some sand into his beautiful coat. At least he did not attempt to eat this silly thing, nor did he attempt to make us a gift of it.

Our quiet beach setting also provided us with an excellent location to observe the other miracles of nature that took place there. Once every year, the sea turtles would make their beach invasion, and crawl through the sand up above the high water mark where they would lay their eggs and cover them with a large mound of sand. Fortunately, the state of Florida has a program that provides protection for this wonderful process by spotting and marking these nests with wooden stakes and ribbons. This keeps humans from disturbing the nests with their all terrain vehicles, and Jeeps, as they run up and down the beach, usually paying little or no attention to the sand that they dig up unless there's a sunbather in their path that doesn't show up on a GPS. Later in the year, when the multitude of tiny turtles try to make their return to the ocean, they have to make their way over the tire tracks, while at the same time avoiding the multitude of sea birds that are intent on picking them off as they wobble to the safety of the water.

In January and February it is possible to sight "Right Whales" about two hundred yards off the shoreline, as they bring their young newborn calves to warmer water from the New England birthing waters. There are only about 300 of these beautiful creatures left, and Gwen and I have spotted them on two occasions. They are often accompanied by a cluster of dolphins, that all frolic together perhaps helping each other in the feeding process. The baby whales are six to eight feet long and it is a magnificent sight to see. Professional whale watchers are able to identify them by the markings and sometimes scars on their immense bodies. They are also tracked by airplanes, as well as volunteers up and down the coast that report their sightings in order to have them recorded.

Our location also provided us with a prime view of the NASA space vehicles as they blast off over the ocean. The launches were always spectacular, especially those at night. Cape Canaveral is about 50 or so miles south, and can also be reached easily by automobile. Another interesting natural phenomenon in this area of the beach that is related to the seasonal changes that occur with the sand and the Coquina rocks that pepper the shoreline.

During the winter season on our particular one-mile stretch, the beautiful but sharp edged rocks are wonderful havens for all manner of tiny sea creatures, however they do not allow any access to the beautiful water. Only the reddish, coarse combination of sand and crushed seashells are visible interspersed with the coquina rocks. In the summer season, the tides with their awesome relentless motion, actually take the finer sand from the sand bars that lie beyond the rocks, and move them in towards the beach, one grain at a time! Over a period of a few weeks, the lighter sand completely covers the rocks and the entire beach, with a firm layer over the red coarse sand below. This process makes it possible to even ride bicycles on the sand, which was not something that could be accomplished when the sand was softer. Then when the season changes, the rocks reappear and white sand returns to recreate the sand bars. It is so very difficult for us as humans to really understand and appreciate the wonders of Nature that surround us in our everyday lives and we certainly do not think nearly enough about the ways that we are destroying these miracles in so many foolish ways. It makes me wonder if our future generations of Grand and Great grandchildren will be able to enjoy the natural beauty that you and I take so much for granted.

CHAPTER 18

Vermont Calls

As much as we enjoyed our life near the beach, and the dogs had a perfect environment to frolic in, it was important to return to Vermont for a portion of the summer, as Florida is very hot and humid in July, August, and September. When we reached Vermont and put the pups out to pasture in the beautiful collection of pine trees, white birch, oaks and maples. We were not in Vermont long before I noticed that Prince was not moving as easily as he normally did, and had a slight limp. He did not seem to be in any distress, however it was better to be careful, and I called our dear Vet buddies, Brad and Angela. When I got Prince into the familiar office, and he had a chance to sniff every inch of the waiting area to determine whether or not any of his friends had visited here lately, we sat and waited for our turn.

When Brad got Prince weighed (now about eighty pounds), and up onto the examining table, it didn't take long for him to take Prince's right rear leg, and rotate it in various directions, and declare it a bit loose, which in lay terms meant that he had injured a ligament in his knee. We are always hearing about ACL damage in athletes, in particular football and hockey players. Our own daughter Debby had done a job on her knee playing hockey at the University of Vermont, so we knew that surgery was the only answer. Brad recommended a surgeon in the nearest town, so an appointment was made for the next week. Prince, of course had no idea what this was all about, but was going to know soon. The orthopedic Vet completed his exam and explained that Prince had torn the anterior cruciate ligament on his right leg, and in fact would need an operation to repair not only the right leg, but the left one as well.

Where was my Canine Medicare when I needed it? I knew I should have purchased some sort of medical insurance for pets, especially when I found out that the cost would be $1800, and I knew that Prince was neutered and could never pay his way by siring a new litter of Golden babies. However, just looking into those beautiful big brown eyes, I knew that this was a small price to pay in order to get my big buddy back to a normal healthy condition.

Prince stayed overnight in the clinic, and when I returned the next afternoon, I found him with both of his rear legs fairly devoid of fur, and covered with dressings to protect his sutures. I was told that for the next week I should place a sling under his body to support him as he took care of his body functions. Old Dr. Jim would have liked to see me holding up Prince's rear end as we looked for a suitable place to squirt. The surgeon told me that there was a screw placed on each leg in order to attach the ligament, but that he should be able to have complete mobility in a short time. I could feel the screws under the tissue when I stroked his leg, but he recovered quickly and was normal except that his running gait seemed altered but functional.

Angel, of course, probably wondered what on earth had happened to her brother since his appearance had changed dramatically, and there were some new and different medicinal odors present when she sniffed his large bandages. It did not take long for all of this excitement to pass, and when Prince was visited by his three-legged cousin Parker, they had something in common to talk about. They had both done their part to perpetuate the canine orthopedic practice, but with good results.

One of the reasons why summers in Vermont are enjoyable is the proximity of a varied assortment of animals that inhabit the property. Several years ago, a large moose had roamed through the backyard, but could find no playmates, so he kept on heading north, and may be back in Maine by now. It was usually our plan to head south before October, however this year's circumstances led to a stay that included half of October. This change made it possible to witness the glorious panorama of fall foliage colors, and it is never really disappointing. There is a view from our living room that extends for twenty miles to the mountains of New Hampshire, and there are approximately 100 apple trees on the property that are just now being properly maintained. This group of trees has made the area a very popular meeting place for many of the white tail deer and other critters. Unfortunately, the deer, though beautiful and graceful, cause a great deal of damage to the flower gardens, trees and shrubs in the yard. They look at you from a distance of 20-30 yards with their large doe eyes as they munch on your favorite flowers, most of which will die from the frost anyway. It is good that they didn't start eating the garden in early summer, because it could start a motion to have a year-round deer season.

Most of the deer present are does of varying sizes and their pretty baby spotted fawns, with an occasional spike horn buck. This October a nice 6 point buck appeared for the first time, shortly before dark and just after the flock of does had had their fill of the fallen apples. Although the deer have always been present in this location, a few more characters from Jonah's Ark started to appear in numbers that caused my wife to refer to our place as "Butz' Zoo". During the late afternoon, 20 large turkeys started to make the yard their browsing area, and made me begin to wonder if I should pick up my old shotgun and find out if native Vermont Turkey is really as tasty as a Butterball from the grocery store. Gwen nixed the idea because she was pretty sure that the feathers do not fall out of the plump-bodied turkey as it draws its last breath on earth. It was probably a good thought as I hadn't hunted for a few years, and would be quite embarrassed if my marksmanship were faulty.

Over a period of two weeks, there were daily visits by the aforementioned, but to top that all off, my wife spotted a large fearless, spiked, object in the top of a now leafless apple tree. Fortunately the dogs were not outside because that would present a large problem for any unsuspecting canine, as a Porcupine rarely loses a battle. This big fat guy had climbed the tree nearly to the top in his quest for the apples, and the branches bent precariously over as he sat there looking down at me while I snapped his photo.

The icing on the cake for our menagerie came as we sat in our dining room with dear friends, "the Adelbergers," visiting from Pennsylvania, having breakfast. This dining room is mostly glass in order to better enjoy the beautiful wooded scenery in front of us. As we sat and talked about old times, a moving dark object flashed past the corner of my eye, and I realized that there was a bear walking across my backyard only 50 feet from the house. I jumped up in disbelief, as I had never seen any real black bear in the wild even though I had hunted deer in Maine and Vermont for twenty-five years.

While Gwen and our thrilled company watched, I had to run down stairs to retrieve the camera that usually was upstairs! (That's normal procedure eh??). By the time that I was able to get the camera in place, it was now evident that this beautiful large "Mama Bear" was accompanied by three broad bottomed black bear cubs. I had heard that there was a bear in the vicinity that was very adept at tearing down bird feeders in many yards, but I couldn't believe that she was here with her whole family. The large fuzzy creature stood on her hind legs, and shook the apple tree to provide treats for her youngsters, and I wondered what would have happened if my porcupine had still been in the tree top.

It was only a matter of five minutes when the whole episode was over and the four bears disappeared into the woods as quickly as they had entered the scene. We probably will not see them again since they have been reported over a 15-mile area. Now that the foliage has passed its peak, and frost would soon kill all of the plants, flowers and shrubs that the deer had not already eaten, it was time to pack the pups up and head for Virginia to visit Parker "The tripod," and our two sons.

All of the pleasure and excitement that we had garnered from this unique bear visitation was dashed when we found out that this Mama bear had been shot by a Massachusetts hunter during the Nov. hunting season. How any dedicated hunter would shoot a mother bear in the presence of her 3 young cubs is beyond my comprehension, and would go a long way towards banning hunting completely on our 5000-acre compound. Everyone who heard about the incident was outraged and could only pray that the 3 small cubs would be able to survive the difficult Vermont frigid winter. We may never find out if the young animals were able to use their natural instincts to get through a long winter season without their mother. I had at least gotten a few good photos of them.

Since this tragic event happened there happened to be a nice series about the life of the American black bear on the TV show "Animal Planet", and it showed how well the mother bear is able to make a den amongst trees and caves where available, in order for her family to survive even the worst weather conditions. When the temperatures venture well below 0 degrees Fahrenheit, as they did this last winter, the chances of very young cubs getting through unscathed without the presence of a large mother bear are not very good.

CHAPTER 19

Not You (Melanoma) Again!

It was a 10-hour drive to Va. And without a van to hold the two dogs, clothing, Vermont cheddar, computers, and the two old folks we would not have survived. We always tried to keep our visitations down to three or four days, and always took off again toward Florida just about the time that the Golden trio were just getting to have fun together. It was already too cold for Parker to do his swan dive into the pool and Prince and Angel would not get close enough to the water to even get splashed. There were deer here all over the place, and most were kept out by an 8 foot high plastic fence that surrounds the property. There are so many of the "Bambi's" that many landowners actually hire a professional deer hunter to keep the numbers down. The venison gathered from these hunts is given to needy families in the area, and the risk of running your car into the deer at night is greatly reduced. The herds grow so quickly that the food supply simply cannot maintain them. So the thinning out process actually makes them healthier, but maybe not happier!

Just as we packed up to continue the trek back to Florida, my son John mentioned that since Parker was alone and getting older, that when we came back to Vermont next summer he would like to add another Golden puppy to our family. We all would look forward to that process since we were now all getting to be retriever experts.

After another twelve-hour drive, we again arrived at home base, and when unpacked could resume our daily jaunts on the beach. It is always funny to watch the two "Sniffers" going back to revisit an interesting scent source even though they had just examined it the day before. As humans, I guess we simply can't really understand how important it is to have such acute sensory perceptions that nothing gets past them, from a treat hidden in your pocket, to an explosive in a terrorist suitcase. I often wondered if their noses ever wore out after 10-12 years of scent analysis. I am sure that the world is a safer place when these wonderful animals can detect drugs, bombs and even deeply buried avalanche victims.

Whenever we visited the beach, the two dogs usually always stayed in close proximity to each other, but would sometimes separate themselves from us by as much as one quarter of a mile. They would still be in viewing range, but could not hear us call, mainly because the surf always made noise. There were at that time no private homes on that stretch of the beach, so there were no real distractions that would prevent them from returning to our side. Prince, being larger than Angel was always faster and his range was far greater than hers, but he didn't bring us back any presents unless you consider a rotted fish carcass a suitable gift!

One day, Angel was very slow in her return, and upon examining her right rear paw, I discovered why she had been limping. One of her paws was swollen, and at first I thought that she had an infected claw, or had torn it loose running through the multitude of sharp shells and other debris that one encounters on every beach. It is amazing to see the variety of objects that are cast up on the beach by the wave action. Everything from large dead birds, half eaten fish, all sorts of bottles, cans and even a large three foot long wooden case that was a US Navy flare of some kind, that was best left alone. If some of the foolish kids who race their all-terrain vehicles and Jeeps up and down the beaches while slugging down beer had ever come across this box with it's dangerous contents, who knows what might have been the consequence. It did seem that a new unusual object was deposited onto the beach every day, summer and winter. The wind came mostly from the water and the smell of the sand covered seaweed along with the salt water was invigorating as well as healthy. There was no way that we could imagine the thousands of tiny creatures that live above and below the sand and crushed shell beach. You could always sit and dig with a shovel or your bare hand down a foot or so into the beach and come up with something different all of the time. Tiny shells with or without inhabitants, small crabs or objects unknown to non-biologists, were all there in great abundance, even when they were tossed about with each new wave surge.

We decided that Angel needed to see her Florida Vet. in St.Augustine, who was one of four female Vets who had a very nice clinic there. Angel was now six years old, and her minor skin conditions were really the only medical problems that she had exhibited.

Prince, of course went with us to the clinic, and was very upset when we took her into the clinic building without him, since they usually had veterinary visits together. When the attractive young female veterinarian met us in the waiting room of a beautiful, well-equipped clinic, I couldn't help compare it to the home office that Dr. Jim had run for forty years. Things had really changed, and now more than 50 percent of veterinarians are female. However, the level of competence, and the love of animals had not been diminished by the generational differences. Upon examination, the doctor decided that the entire toe needed to be removed, and a biopsy would be done to enable her to proceed with treatment.

We left the office with a well-padded right rear foot, which Prince sniffed and licked when we placed angel in the back of the van. He, as always, was overjoyed to be reunited with her, and we both hoped that neither of them would try to help the healing process by chewing off the bandages so as to be able to lick the wound in a way that was natural for them. We were able to keep the area covered, and awaited the phone call to advise us of the diagnosis.

Early the next day, the phone rang, and we were told that our baby Angel's toe had been found to be a melanoma. I was shocked since I had never thought of this cancer as one that affects animals and humans alike. There are several skin cancer conditions that all merit attention, such as basal cell carcinoma, squamous cell carcinoma, and Xanthoma, however, none of these has the ability to cause death if untreated to the degree that melanoma does. It has been my experience that the average person has no clue what a melanoma is, or how to help prevent it, or that it does not at the present time have any cure once this growth attains a certain depth. It had not crossed my mind that melanoma comes from melanin which gives skin its color, and almost all humans and animals have this substance in their bodies. I have had three melanomas since I was 55 years old! If you learn nothing else from this book, please pay attention to the next few sentences.

We all have skin cells called melanocytesl, that make melanin that protects the deeper layers of skin from the sun's rays. If melanocytes are exposed to ultraviolet light they may grow abnormally, and create a cancerous melanoma. However, excess sun exposure is not the only cause, as melanoma can occur anywhere on the body, even areas that have never seen the sunlight. That is the scary part of this dreaded disease.

Remember the ABCDE of melanoma. A—asymmetry—one side is different than the other side. B—the borders have uneven edges, notched or blunted. C—color—uneven areas of red, blue, brown, tan, pink, white, and gray. D—diameter—usually more than one-quarter inch in diameter, E—evolution—change shape, color, size, quickly.

Now that Angel had surprised us with this complication in our life, we had only to hope and pray that this surgery would take care of it. For the next few months however, Angel seemed to have less energy and her beach walks became shorter and less exciting for her. She did continue to deliver a starfish on occasion, since it was her favorite. At first, she was still enjoying her food, and was sleeping more than usual, however we attributed that to growing older. Sometimes she still had that sad look in her eyes, if only we would have realized what that portended. We loved her so much, and we had never lost a Golden under 10 years old, and even old Squire reached the grand old age of 14.

After two more months of watching her slow all activities, it was necessary to return to the clinic to find out if this was related to her melanoma. Once again we piled the two siblings into the van, but this time I had to gently lift Angel into the rear seat. When we arrived, Angel was able to walk, albeit slowly, into the waiting room, but she had no interest in sniffing around the room (not a good sign!). Prince was very distressed by having to remain in the car, and expressed himself by barking excitedly, which was very rare for him. The young Vet took Angel back to the examining room, and after going over her body with her gentle hands she had a detectable distressed look on her face which needed no explanation. She did however maintain her cheerful manner, and told us that it would be best to leave Angel there overnight, and enable her to do a thorough examination to determine a course of action. Then Gwen and I both leaned down over Angel as she lay quietly on the table, and hugged her, while kissing her sweet face, not wanting to believe that this would probably will be the final time that we would have physical contact with our "Lover Dog".

We walked back to the car and settled Prince down, as he tried to find Angel. Perhaps knowing somehow that something was wrong, terribly wrong! When we arrived home, Prince wouldn't eat any food as he roamed the backyard looking in vain for his sister. In about two hours, we received the call that neither of us wanted, but knew would come. The vet explained that the melanoma had spread to the lungs exactly the same way as it does with human victims of this insidious cancer, and that there was nothing that could be done to save her. We instructed her to put her down and that we appreciated everything that she had been able to do, and could tell from her voice that she was also deeply saddened by this turn of events. I lay down on the floor with Prince between Gwen and I and held him close as tears welled up in the eyes of both of us.

We were sure that Prince understood that now he was our only remaining canine family member. We could only try to recall the multitude of times that Angel had given us her unconditional love along with countless pleasure filled moments that only a dog can provide. I shall always remember her as perhaps the most loving of all the dogs that help make up my "50 Golden years." I should not make that statement, because Prince Too had the same gene pool as Angel, but she passed on at such a young age that she must have tried to pack ten years of love into a six-year life.

CHAPTER 20

Full Circle

Life continued even without Angel, and Prince did his best to become the new "Velcro Dog." We still kept our schedule of scouring the beaches for gold doubloons while waiting for our ship to come in, and Prince was just starting to enjoy venturing into the foamy ocean as long as one of us was waist deep with a treat in hand. It was difficult for him to understand why the waves made so much noise and continued to crash in and then subside with no apparent good reason. He did however, seem to enjoy the cooling effect that his immersion in the water was providing him. I am not sure if the salt water that he inadvertently swallowed gave him as much pleasure as he derived from licking your hand or arm.

Unfortunately, the beautiful mile long stretch of the ocean-front was beginning to show subtle signs of inevitable change as multimillion dollar 3 story palaces started to rise from the sand. The homes were not going up fast, but four 10-12 floor luxury condominiums were stretching skyward day by day, as hundreds of helmeted construction guys and girls were seen scampering all over the "Cement skeletons." I marveled each day at the mammoth 14 story high cranes that were on top of steel towers that measured only 10-12 feet across at their base.

The homes and the condominium buildings were only 20-30 yards from the high water mark on the beach and were constructed with so much steel and cement that it would take a severe hurricane to inflict much damage to any of them. The first home to be constructed on our mile long beach was designed and built by a well known architect and it would have taken an earthquake to budge it, and the views from every room in the entire house were breathtaking. When you added the fact that you could also walk a short distance to be on the first tee of a magnificent seaside links style golf course, it was not difficult to be a little envious.

During the long period of construction Prince, Gwen and I walked past the home almost every day on the beach and would venture onto the walkway that led to the pool area to see what new construction had occurred since our last visit. One thing always brought me back to reality, and that was the fact that the monthly electric bill for this palace would consume my entire Social Security check!

A few hundred yards up the beach to the north was the area where the 3 new 10-12 story luxury condominiums were being built. These sites were crawling with construction workers performing a mind-boggling array of physical tasks some of which were quite dangerous. It was unimaginable to me that a human body would climb hundreds of steel steps up to his little "Office in the sky," a cabin in the middle of the crane that had a big pile of cement blocks on one end, and a long steel extension, holding the pulleys that would support the cables with their buckets of cement on the other end. I couldn't help but wonder if the operator had a toilet up there in the sky, or scampered up and down all of those rungs two or three times a day to relieve himself. I was sure of one thing, his weekly wage probably made my Social Security check look like small change, but I know that he deserved every bit of it. The view that the operator had from this lofty perch must be spectacular, as he looked out over the beautiful blue and green Atlantic Ocean with occasional whales and dolphins on one side, and the splendid green golf course dotted with large white sand traps on the other. On his lunch breaks, if he stayed up there, he could have entertained himself by checking out the small groups of tiny golfers with a pair of binoculars. "Big brother on the links" might have embarrassed a few golfers who were moving balls from behind trees or kicking them slyly out of sand traps, if they were ever reported.

After five years of enjoying this "Golf Paradise," with the ocean to boot, my loving companion realized that the many close friends that we had left behind at Innisbrook were dearer to us than we had realized, and that maybe we should consider returning to our old "Stomping ground." Since my dreams of catching fish every day never did come to fruition, and my golf game was unchanged, it was not a difficult decision to move

Prince Too and his surrounding pieces of furniture back to the West Coast and Innisbrook. Since our moving company boss had become a fairly close personal friend, due to our frequent moves we did not hesitate to call him back. We had moved only twice in our first 40 years of married life, and now in the last ten years our belongings no longer had any idea where they were supposed to be.

In many ways the Ocean-Golf location was the one that I had always considered ideal, and although it was aesthetically nearly perfect, it lacked the cozy "old friends" type of environment that we really needed to exist happily at our age. As far as Prince Too was concerned, he could have taken up residency in the local landfill as long as he had us in sight and in petting range.

When my old friend Drake the mover, arrived to remove us from the house that he had just set us up in five years earlier, he was surprised that I could leave a nice two story house with a double garage, and try to fit all of its contents into a second story three bedroom condo. He had a point, and he and his helpers were the happy beneficiaries of many items that we could no longer use or had no room for. I am sure that he and his crew would have liked to move us once a year! This included items ranging from fishing rods and reels to a king-size bed. Perhaps the biggest change for me was going to have to live without a garage for the first time since I was in the Air Force. I had almost forgotten all of the heartaches that our garage fire had caused in Woodstock 30 years earlier, but a man and a car really need a shelter to store all of our crap. Wives also need room to keep gardening items and lawn chairs along with bicycles purchased with the noble intention of keeping ourselves fit.

When the truck was fully loaded with some items tied precariously onto the rear end we were about to head west! The moving crew was happy to have a 4-hour ride to enable them to regain their strength. As I emerged from the empty house, I called Blake over and said that I forgot to tell him about the array of packed boxes that were stored in my neighbor's garage! I had been packing them for weeks and had the extra garage about 1/2 full of various sized cardboard boxes. The poor guy was nearly overcome by this new revelation, but being a veteran mover he quickly adapted to the situation.

While he and his three helpers took a break, I dashed off to the nearest U-Haul truck depot that was only a few miles away and was able to quickly lease a medium sized truck that would hold the remaining load. You would not believe how fast that we packed this baby up as I tried to do double duty since I felt responsible for the mistake. Everyone but the drivers drank a celebrity beer and the procession took off. Gwen, Prince Too and I followed in our fully loaded van. What a relief!

When the movers found out that our new move was going to a second floor condo with no elevators, we almost destroyed our nice friendship. I still marvel at the fact that they hand-carried two items up the back two level narrow stairway that they were sure must have been entirely filled with either lead ingots or beach sand. One was a four-drawer 48-inch wide, 5-foot tall filing cabinet that had been accidentally locked and was completely full of heavy folders, papers and photo albums. I didn't find the key until a week later, but I didn't think that it was necessary to call them to tell them how easy it would have been to move those drawers one at a time. It is a good thing that our relationship had been enhanced by the aforementioned gifts, in addition to a good tip.

The second item was a nice old antique dental cabinet, the kind with about 20 various sized drawers into which I had carefully stockpiled every kind of screw, bolt, nail and other heavy, but small hardware items. If it had been much larger, I could have easily opened up an addition to the local "Ace hardware store." But the sturdy lads assured me that it would be "no problem," and sure enough managed to get this antique up to it's resting place in one piece. It must have weighed at least 300 pounds! As I was praising them for their great ability and strength, they coyly inquired if there might be a baby grand or a large safe that they could further impress me with before they went home? I assured them that this was the last move until the nursing home got us, and by then we wouldn't need much besides a medicine chest, a few canes and a "Porta potty."

Now that we were back on the west coast of Florida, and unburdened by the multitude of problems that accompany home ownership, we could now really enjoy the retirement life of the "Golden years." Prince adapted to the new environment quite easily since all we had to do was walk down a flight of stairs and find ourselves on the fairway of one of our four golf courses. Innisbrook is a Golf and Tennis resort that consists of 25 separate condominium lodges that each contain an assortment of one, two and three bedrooms suites, and three buildings that are three bedroom permanent residences, and do not allow rentals. The whole complex is located on approximately 1000 acres and has recently been purchased by "Salamander Inc. The new owner Sheila Johnson is a leader in the world of hospitality and entertainment.

This new ownership is responsible for the four golf courses, seven swimming pools, several restaurants, and a group of convention buildings that cater to large meetings of all kinds. The PGA golf tour holds a tournament here in early spring. There is something for every one here and more is being made available by the new ownership in the next year. Needless to say there is always something to do, however the property also lends itself well to the needs of some of its older members who wish to enjoy a quiet life style

We live on the fairway of a beautiful par five hole where Prince, now recovered from the loss of Angel, or at least we think he has, can run or walk over a large area of grass covered hills lined with a variety of palms, oaks, cypress, and pines. He particularly enjoys running at full speed and diving on to the carpet of lawn while flipping over onto his back to wriggle about to relieve his back itches, real or imagined. Since we have a large flock of Canada Geese that also roam the fairways, we have an inordinate amount of "Goose do do," that he has to maneuver around. Because of the fact that he does not always avoid these droppings, I have tried to teach him to chase the beautiful large birds, with no potty training, on to another part of the course and they don't usually return for a week or so.

Although I had never had success with training Prince to locate golf balls, I did enjoy having him along side of me on what I call my "15 ball walk" or on some occasions, my "60 ball walk." Innisbrook courses are usually played by visitors who for the most part have no interest in seeing, or worse yet encountering, either a snake or a 10 foot alligator, most of which have "squatters rights" in all of our ponds and swamp areas. Since I have had a passion for ball hawking for forty years, I have developed a few basic rules to follow. Rule 1: states that there is no place on the golf course that you can't find a ball that is the result of an errant shot. Rule II: if there is one ball in that location, there could be another very close, sometimes in contact, and rule III, adopted from an old Chinese proverb, "man who holds head high, find no golf ball." It is imperative that while trekking for Titleists you need to always keep one eye looking for a tiny white, sometimes partially buried, round object, while the other eye scans the immediate area for a coiled form that usually represents a snake whose territory you may be violating.

To be quite honest, I have seen very few snakes over the years of traversing through their territory, and firmly believe that they're more afraid of you than we are of them. This is even true of large alligators, though I have trouble convincing friends from the north that this is the case. All in all it is best to respect these creatures and attempt not to aggravate them. Stepping on them comes under the category of aggravation, and is not recommended. If you make enough noise with your feet, it will give them ample time to slither away, and they do.

The pond that is nearest to our condo attracts a large number of water birds that take flight as Prince approaches, but he doesn't normally like to chase them. He was particularly interested when three otters appeared cruising around in the pond while watching the dogs' every move. When he moved to the far side of the pond, they would slip out of the water, shake their sleek bodies as if to tease him, and if he made a move in their direction would fly back into the dark water with hardly a ripple showing where they entered. Although the otters are a great joy to watch, they are real fish killers, and can clean out all of the fish in a pond in a short time. The Cormorants are fish eating large birds that have the most beautiful royal blue eyes that are not usually seen since they won't allow you to get that close. These birds can fish out a lake when they gather 20 or more as a group at one end of the water, and all submerge in order to swim the length of the pond grabbing all unwary fish along the way.

The only more efficient method of using Cormorants to fish is the method used in Asia, particularly China, where the birds have a tether attached to a leg, and a steel ring placed around the slender neck which allows the bird to catch the fish, but prevents them from swallowing it. Very frustrating for the bird, but it works out especially well when the owner takes a small wooden raft out onto the river at night, and attracts the fish with a bright light. He hopes to bring the unsuspecting "Pisces" near to the boat so the fisherman can dump his "Fisher bird" into the water to grab the prey. I often wondered if these birds could be taught to bring up golf balls from the murky bottom of the lake. I would most likely get a bitter letter from an animal rights group in this country, but not in the orient where most anything goes when it comes to survival.

Prince Too 2000

Prince Too
2005

Prince Too
2005

CHAPTER 21

It's A Good Life

In the spring of 2006, I came upon an ad for the "Florida Good Life Games" for the County of Pinellas, in Florida. This area covers cities like Clearwater, Palm Harbor, Dunedin, Largo, Tarpon Springs and St. Petersburg. The population is just under one million people. The Good Life Games are held every spring, and are a form of Olympics for men and women from 50 years up. The competition is divided into five-year groups, such as 50-54,55-59, all the way to Methuselah. The activities range from individual events in baseball, golf, baseball, track and field, to badminton. Almost every sport is involved. There are even team games such as Basketball and Softball.

Since everyone likes to think of himself or herself as a potential decathlon champion, I decided to look into this a little more closely. The old saying, "The older I get, the better I was," comes to mind. I filled out an application with entries in 13 events and intentionally left out the 100-yard dash, and the one-mile run. At the age of 77, those events would have led to a visit to the intensive care unit. I did however, have golf, baseball and track and field to consider. I recalled that I had thrown shotput, discus and javelin in high school with some success, and how many of my senior citizen friends could even lift up a shotput, let alone throw it past their shadow. I really did not want to put off trying these games because every year seems to bring new physical disabilities to nearly everyone.

I decided that some practice was in order, so I got on the Internet to watch films of various track and field events. Since I did not have any of the required equipment, I had to innovate, so I made a discus out of a barbell weight that also served as a shot put. Then I made a javelin out of some old curtain rods, and was ready to go. Prince Too was my trainer and coach, as we went out to our backyard golf fairway. He watched me throw this motley group of pseudo athletic devices, and fortunately decided not to retrieve any of them. It would have been sad if I had bonked him with a 10 or12 pound iron weight which he could have interpreted as a plastic Frisbee.

Since progress was a little slow, and sometimes painful, I decided to visit our local high school track to observe the guys and girls at their practice. The coach was very nice as he let me use their real equipment, and give me some tips. They do not have javelin competition in most high schools, as there is considerable risk to throwing spears! Now if only my rotator cuff didn't give out, I might be ready for the real competition. I had already decided to forego the high jump and the pole vault, as it would have required some jet assistance to launch this 210-pound missile. As I practiced with coach Prince on the fairway behind my condo, some of the worker bees from golf maintenance stopped by to find out why I was heaving an old 8 foot curtain rod back and forth on the golf fairway. They also noticed that my makeshift discus was actually taking bigger divots than a 36-handicap novice golfer, and suggested that I should really use it only in the rough.

The various events were held over a one-month span which allowed we older geeks to recover from muscle spasms, and tendonitis. When I arrived with Prince at the first Track and Field event, the first thing that I noticed was that some of the participants were pulling little kids' wagons that contained their own personal shot puts, discus, and javelins along with changes of clothing and even shoes. When I then found out that one of these "walking sports stores," was in my division, any visions of Olympic medals quickly vanished. As it turned out, I was able to beat this dude in two events which by itself made the whole adventure worthwhile. This particular well-tanned gentleman was the current National Champion in the 74-79 age group for the high jump, and was very competitive in most all of the events.

The winners of the events were then eligible to compete in the Florida State championships, and then on to the National Good Life Games. The National Good Life games are held every two years around the country. The entire event was both interesting and uplifting, as I was able to see men and women from 50-100 years old competing. One gentleman in the 95-year-old golf event was as happy as he would have been if there had been any other participants. I saw a 65-year-old man who had polio, and was enjoying the competition even though his broad jump attempt only yielded him a 24-inch jump, and he was applauded. There were several 70-80-year old ladies competing in the soccer ball kick and football throw. Some people never do grow old, and this was one of the reasons why. When the events were all over, I was able to receive a few of the medals that hung from the red, white and blue ribbons, and were quite attractive.

I gave them all to the grandchildren.

Tally—Parker 2007

Parker "Tripod"
2007

CHAPTER 22

Parker's New Pal

As each summer came, the amount of time that we would spend in Vermont seemed to grow shorter. This was true even though I would prefer to spend more time in Vermont, as the life style there at our somewhat remote location was to be envied. I could spend more time building stonewalls, and trimming the surrounding woodland at a schedule that suited me very well. We were slowly but surely adapting to the summer months of June and July in Florida, but didn't want to miss at least a few months of time in Vermont. The travel from Vermont to Florida on mostly Interstate highways gets a little more hectic as the years pass. This year's trek to the North would give us a chance to visit the latest addition to our "50 Golden Years," as our oldest son, John had just acquired a beautiful female Golden pup to make sure that good old Parker didn't get to act like a couch potato.

The newcomer named "Tally," came from Vermont and had a lighter shade of golden coat similar to Parker. Her vim and vigor would add a bit of spice to the life of the now aging old warrior. From the time I first saw "Tally" run, I was convinced that she was the fastest Golden that I had ever seen. She was relentless and fearless when it came to retrieving any object that was thrown, and I was afraid that on many occasions that she would run directly into the two foot high stone wall that I had built in the yard. She miraculously avoided the barrier with a last-minute leap that is so instinctive that it could not be taught. She had a vertical leap of at least two feet, who said that "White dogs can't jump!"

Whenever a tennis ball was sent into the air, Tally would be half way to it before our tripod buddy "Parker" even figured out where the darn thing was headed. She would have the ball in her mouth ready for another throw of 20-30 yards before he moved 10 yards. At least he was up to trying, but he was happy to make a 15-foot effort at another ball after she had rocketed by him. Sometimes she was able to grab the long initial throw, and be back in time to grab his ball before he was able to pick it up. I think that he was very frustrated by this action, but he never complained. Since she could only hold two balls in her mouth at once, it was sometimes necessary to have three tennis balls in action at the same time, in order for him to be successful. It was very pleasurable to watch these guys retrieve, just as long as you did not get into their way. They could easily knock over any adult person that stood in the way of their ultimate goal of speedy ball retrieval. After about thirty minutes of this furious action, it was time for them to return to the house with their large pink tongues almost reaching the ground, and very much in need of a bowl of water. They would soon be fast asleep since apparently most dogs sleep more than they are in a conscious state. I even know some humans that go through life in a similar manner!

Neither Prince Too nor Angel had ever really had a penchant for chasing and retrieving thrown objects; perhaps there was a missing gene in their otherwise perfect configurations. Prince frequently would run to the object that had been thrown, and then instead of taking it up gently and returning it to the original owner, he would lie down with this thing planted between his outstretched legs. No sort of prompting would be effective enough to give him reason to believe that he should take any action other than guarding the ball or whatever it was.

However, Prince was able to allow our friends to attend the demonstration of what it means for a dog to have a "soft mouth," an absolute requirement for the retriever breeds No duck, or pheasant hunter would ever want to have a tug of war with his working dog over the bird that had just been knocked out of the air by a perfect shot. Even though I had never hunted birds, I know that once he had gotten over the frightening sound of a 12-gauge shotgun blast over his head, that Prince would gladly hand over the limp recipient of the lead pellets without a battle. In order to prove his ability to perform a task like that, I frequently at cocktail parties, would have Prince sit squarely in front of me while I placed a small piece of pretzel or soda cracker in my mouth with only one half inch of it protruding past my incisors. At my signal, as I leaned down towards him, he would deftly remove the pretzel or whatever from my mouth without even touching me. This gentle 80-pound dog had to turn his head at an angle in order to reach under my slightly oversized proboscis so that I would suffer no bodily injury. I had seen many dogs of all sizes that I would not attempt that feat with. Although I am not a Jimmy Durante look alike, my recently deceased best friend from college used to chide me by remarking that I was the only person he knew that could smoke a cigarette in the shower without it going out. I retorted by adding that, "at least it wasn't a cigar."

After I'd performed the pretzel trick a few times, my trusty accomplice would simply crawl under the coffee table in amongst the guests, and await the second show. Now that Prince didn't have his Angel to keep him company, even to sleep at night in contact with each other, he usually did his "Velcro" action with me. Even in our condo if I would move to another room, I would be joined by him quietly keeping me constantly in his sight. He loved Gwen and I every bit as much as we loved him, and you could see it in his sparkling brown eyes.

CHAPTER 23

The Final Curtain

Prince was ten years old on the seventh of February 2006, as I reflected on the fact that unfortunately, larger breeds of dogs in general do not enjoy the longer life expectancy that their smaller canine contemporaries do. Back in Vermont our oldest dog, Squire had managed to live to the grand old age of 14, while all of the others exited our world in an average of 10-11 years. Angel of course, was the exception when she died prematurely at six, which was an anomaly. While still living in Vermont full time, I had a patient who was German born, and of course, had a German dog named Fritz, who was a shorthaired Dachshund. One day I needed to return a borrowed item to their home nearby, and really did not even know that they had dogs at all. As I left my car, and approached their house, I was greeted by a hearty bark that was being uttered from this little walking hot dog that was about 18 inches long and 8-10 inches high. After I was advised that he was not the "Killer Dog" that his appearance suggested, I leaned down to pet the little old protector of their homestead.

I remember that Dachshunds are really good hunting dogs even though he didn't look as if he could bite anything other than your ankle. As I stroked his long head, I couldn't help but notice that his tongue just drooped out of one side or the other, and it never appeared to withdraw into his mouth. As heads were in a dentists' bailiwick, I asked the owner if Fritz had a medical condition that resulted in his sagging tongue? Oscar the owner laughed and said, "Hey Jack you are supposed to be the dentist here aren't you?" So I replied that I was guilty of that, but I had never had anyone in my office that exhibited that unusual behavior. Oscar then leaned down to Fritz's level, and reached into his mouth with his fingers so that he could let me look into the old boy's mouth that was completely devoid of any teeth. When a dog is toothless it is then impossible to hold the ever-moving tongue inside of the head, therefore out it pops. The same problem does not seem to happen with humans as their tongues flop around for other reasons.

Prince Too had his two knee operations in his first year, and had never had any repercussions from that operation. He still had the mobility to be able to race about when the spirit was willing. When we took our golf course walks, he never ventured far from me as I did not want him to get near the lakes, as alligators do attack smaller animals and even an 80 pound dog could be dragged into the water from the shore, but is not a likely occurrence. Small dogs have been swept off their feet by the lightning fast action of a gator's tail. Once in the water there are not many creatures that can hold their own with an alligator that is in his element.

However, when you consider the huge number of alligators in Florida, not including those at University of Florida, the number of attacks is statistically very low. Yeah, right! Tell that to the lady who lost her Pomeranian to a big green critter whose nickname is "Chomp!" Now having said that, there are always snakes to consider as dangers to life and limb. But when you live in Florida you must be cognizant of the fact that these hazards do exist.

When it comes to medicines for dogs or humans, all kinds of problems seem to arise. I remember that almost every Golden that I ever owned had the unique ability to eat an entire bowl of dry food kibbles with a tiny pill of medicine hiding in the middle of it, and when the food was all devoured, the miniscule tablet lay in the middle of the dish untouched. How do they do that?

On another occasion, Prince had been having a real bout with diarrhea from who knows what he swallowed, and for two nights he would approach my bed at 2-3 A.M., and just pant while murmuring a soft pleading whimper. This quiet but effective signaling of distress was far better than finding a mess in the middle of a beige Berber carpet. His eyes were pleading with me to hurry and get me out to the wide expanse of golf course fairway, or we would both be sorry! The darkness outside made it impossible to examine the stool to see if I could identify the source of the problem, but we needed to at least stop the flow.

In the morning, I dialed Vermont to get expert advice from Vets, Brad and Angela, as to how to solve this problem. It is difficult to diagnose over the phone, but only a few things are all purpose. Brad asked me if I had any Pepto-Bismol in my mini-pharmacy, and if I did, just try to get a bunch of it into Prince's mouth as quickly as possible, but be sure to take him outside to administer the magical pink fluid.

The significance of this advice was lost on me at the time, however, I led Prince down the stairway to the edge of the sidewalk and attempted to get some of this stuff into his mouth. He did not seem to understand that this was entirely for his benefit, so he ducked and weaved his head about attempting to evade the colorful medication. After a few times, I decided to just allow him to keep his teeth clenched while I pulled his cheek to one side and slid the bottle into the small opening and poured the liquid in.

A moment later, he determined that this stuff did not satisfy his taste buds, so he shook his large shaggy head with as much force as he could muster, and I was the unexpected recipient of a foamy spray of the world's finest antacid. Pink stuff was all over my face, all over my clothing, and covered a good section of the sidewalk. Surprisingly, he did not spread much of it on himself, but now I understood Brad's words of caution as to the site for the medical application. It took two weeks for the pink spots to wash off of the sidewalk, however the benefits promised to Prince were almost immediate as he recovered in a little over a day. I never did determine the cause of the problem, but you can be sure that we now always keep a good supply of this medication close at hand.

Prince did not resist having a leash on, but I am sure that like most animals, he felt happier when he could move about any place unrestricted. When he was in Vermont there was no reason to be contained, and he sniffed his way over acres of land without any consequences. He was somewhat lucky that he did not confront our resident porcupine or a member of the neighboring skunk family. In Florida, since Prince always responded immediately to my call, I seldom burdened him with any form of restraint. Condominium Associations normally have leash laws because they have owners who even feel threatened by a tail wagging Golden Retriever with two tennis balls in his mouth, looking for a friend. Hardly any room left to impart a bite to the visiting stranger. However in this age of litigation, I am sure that everyone is more concerned about being sued than letting any happy dog enjoy his natural tendency to interact with humans.

Unfortunately there are humans who consider a dog of any size, shape, or color, a serious conflict with their sense of well being, and cannot be comfortable when in close proximity to any canine. In my 50 Golden years I never came in contact with one single member of that breed that would even contemplate an attack on the human race for whatever reason.

As it turned out however, my observance of the leash law, or the lack thereof, would cause me great sorrow in the end. Since most retrievers spend half of their life with their noses to the ground, a trait instilled in them from their early ancestors, that included setters and blood hounds. Prince loved to weave in an out of thick clumps of shrubbery around the golf course and the condominiums, usually at the end of our walk.

One of the creatures that loved to live around the shrubs that surround most condos was the ever-present armadillo. These unusual looking critters are found throughout the South and the West. Even though they give the appearance of hard-shelled live armored vehicles, they are in reality fairly soft with a leather feeling to them. They cause no harm except that they dig an enormous amount of holes searching for insects and grubs at night. You could call them useful living golf course aerators if there was just some method to control their errant course of direction. Since they do most of their foraging at night, you don't really see them very often.

One morning as Gwen and I took Prince Too for a morning walk, we encountered a whole fleet of 10-inch long baby armadillos that numbered approximately 6 with their mother. We shall call her "Mother Armadillo," in honor of the large southwestern Spanish culture. The babies were so new that I had to push them off the sidewalk with my foot since they seemed to be fearless or just stupid, and have little interest in us or our monster red dog. After a few gentle kicks they decided that perhaps they were not in their element, so they partly ran and partly wobbled towards a 12-14-inch hole at the base of a large shrub that served as their den. In a matter of seconds they had all disappeared into the mini-cave along with their mother. Prince Too just looked at them as too insignificant to bother with, and we continued on with our morning stroll. They would all return above ground when the sun went down and their Mom would teach them how to make holes in our gorgeous fairway.

One evening as we finished our cruise around the course, looking for a few golf balls, I noticed that he had a slight limp in his gait that I hadn't noticed earlier in the walk. He didn't seem to want to place any weight on his rear right leg, which of course was one of the two rear legs that had undergone the ligament surgery ten years previously. I thought that since he was now ten years old that maybe he was reacting to an area of inflammation, just as I and most of my golfing contemporaries seem to do after a round of golf or a game of tennis.

A few hours later, he seemed to be acting as if he had some pain present, so after moving his leg and eliciting no response, I tried to get a few anti inflammatory pills past his teeth and tongue, however this resulted in his throwing them up. I then placed a call to the local veterinarian that I had used years back when Prince One was still here. He asked me to bring him to the clinic first thing in the morning, and he would examine him more closely. Since Prince did not whimper as I moved his legs into different positions, I thought that waiting until morning would be OK.

During the night, Prince was quite restless, so I was happy when the sun rose in the morning. When I attempted to take him down the stairway his legs would not provide him with the ease of movement that he normally exhibited, but we did reach the van that was only 30 yards away. When we arrived at the vet clinic, we were ushered into an examining room, and there they took Prince back to another room for an X-ray. In less than one-half hour as I petted Prince, who was lying quietly on the table, the Vet came back with the report that the radiographs were normal, but that the blood tests showed that the white blood cell count was extremely high which generally indicates a serious infection. The question was, what could cause such an infection in a relatively short period of time?

The answer would be divulged to us later.

The doctor did note that there was a necrotic (dead tissue) area inside of his rear right leg, but with all his normal fur present, not much could be seen. Since the only way to combat the large amount of infection present was medicine, so he recommended that we start an intravenous antibiotic immediately, and continue it through the night. Before I left the clinic, I placed my arms around my beloved Prince Too, and when our eyes met, I could virtually hear him asking me "Dad, why am I feeling this way? I know that something is very wrong!" Even though tears are rarely present flowing on my face no matter what the situation, I couldn't stop my eyes from showing my pain. We still did not know what was causing this sudden virulent infection, so I had to leave him for the night with the hope that the next day would show some improvement.

As Gwen and I went to bed that night, we both knelt and prayed that God could somehow pull this magnificent, beautiful dog who had helped make our lives so full, through this night of pain. Early the next morning we were awakened by the phone call from the vet who explained that the infection was worse, and that we might consider taking him to Tampa, 30 miles east, to the only intensive care facility for animals that was nearby. There was no guarantee that even this late action would insure that Prince could be saved, especially at his age, and he had suffered so much already that we decided to let him go. We still did not know exactly what had taken Prince from us, and I reflected on the previous day, when I gazed into his soulful eyes, if only he could have told me what had happened. We were to find out three days later.

CHAPTER 24

The Answer

In the condominium that we lived in, there was a gentleman who walked his black and white Springer Spaniel past our porch every day. As he passed below our second story porch, I called down to him and explained to him that Prince Too had died, and that I had a beautiful dog bed that had been given to us by a friend only three months earlier, and that I would like his dog to have it if he didn't already have one. He said that that would be a lovely gift, and so I agreed to drop it off that evening to his condo.

When I got the bed delivered, Jim asked me if we had any idea how Prince had died so suddenly. I told him that we suspected that he was probably bitten by a lethal spider, or more likely a snake. The venomous snake is always a possibility in Florida, however I had not seen a snake of any kind anywhere close to our condo building at any time, even though I saw them often while hunting balls out in the golf course swamps. Snakes, even the poisonous ones do not go about chasing people around even though most of us do not want to give them any chance to prove this point. When they are given enough warning of your presence in their vicinity they will generally quietly move to a different location and you will never know how close they really were. I haven't seen more than 10-15 snakes in the woods and swamps along the golf courses in nearly 30 years of hawking balls, even when the areas that I searched were prime snake habitat.

He hesitated a moment, and then he explained that his grandson, who was visiting, had seen a rattlesnake right outside the building, but didn't know whether to kill it or leave it be. A decision that unfortunately would be a tragic one for our family, however I could not blame him because he had no way of knowing what the consequences would be. Sometimes lives are changed by a seemingly small incident that seems at the time to be somewhat irrelevant.

Now that the mystery was solved, we still had to go on with our lives with out Prince as a part of it, however whenever you accept a dog, or any pet into your life, you must understand that it most likely will predecease you, and you must be prepared for this eventuality. Since we had been through the mourning process about ten times over my 50 Golden years, we were always tremendously saddened by each death, but could never consider it as comparable to the demise of a human being no matter how much that pet had meant to us over its relatively short life. There is not much doubt that the 11 Golden Retrievers that have blessed my life over the years, have played a very important role in the happiness that has been extended to my family and me. This love and joy though great cannot equal the same emotions that are provided to us from our human families that include relatives as well as friends.

I feel sorry for the multitude of folks on this earth, who by choice or chance, have never been able to enjoy the unconditional love and devotion that is supplied to us in the form of a pet, who in my case has always been a beautiful Golden Retriever.

I'm not sure if my wife and I will ever again have one in our home, because of our age, and mobile nature of our lives, however I would not count it out. Whenever I see a Golden walking with a family or sitting majestically in someone's yard, I am compelled to stop whatever I'm doing, and go to the dog in order to get a "Golden Fix" in the form of a warm lick or several strokes on a beautiful silky coat. They will always be a part of our life, present and future, whether they belong to us or some other lucky person.

CHAPTER 25

Golden Resume

The marvelous memories that I had to recall in order to write this story have put me to sleep on innumerable nights over the past few months. Starting with Tawny One in our short military career, which was our exciting entry into the 50 Golden years when he helped us through our early dental practice years when the four children were born. We were exceptionally busy adapting to the rigors of raising the children along with developing the means to support them. As I look back at it now, those days did not seem that different, even though I am sure that they were.

Tawny Two was with us as the children began to grow and became individuals with different personalities and traits. He had no trouble keeping himself occupied, as there was always a youngster around to play with. He of course, made life interesting for us all when he became the sire that produced Missy for us, and the concept that dogs have families also, and that was a wonderful lesson of life for the children as well as for me.

Missy, who became a mother at the tender age of two, altered our lifestyle somewhat, as we needed to learn how to take care of her 9 puppies, that were a delight. However, every who has ever been involved in puppy raising, knows that once the little Golden fuzz balls arrive there are many details that need tending to. First, the children learn how to take care of the new mother, but then the nine accessories also required a great deal of love and patience. The hardest part was yet to come, as they learned that we could not keep all of those cute little critters. There would be some difficult decisions to be made regarding the distribution of our "Little Golden treasures." As often happens, the runt of the litter receives the most compassion from those attending the group, so by acclamation the children all voted to keep the small darker red female who became known as "Tonsils"

This mother daughter combination was such a reflection of love and beauty, as they were constantly together, even through the fire, that all of the children received another healthful life lesson. Over the years each different dog displayed a trait that again showed the children how animals as well as humans, all have virtues that help us to live together in a friendly and useful way.

Then along came Squire, whose physical impairment and ability to overcome it was an important step in the education of the four teenagers. At first Missy died, followed in two years by Tonsils, and poor old Squire was suddenly the only one left to carry out our tradition of Goldens that had now extended over thirty years, so on the stage came Prince One to help Squire live for several more years. If that good old boy had not had the companionship, which included a great deal of teasing with intimidation, there is no doubt that he would have died years earlier. This same phenomenon is also present in the complicated lives of human beings as well. How many people's lives would have been shortened if they had not had the love and companionship of another person to help them through their bad times of stress?

Prince One carried the torch when the Squire passed on and provided us with some of the most interesting episodes of canine misbehavior that we had seen up until that time. Prince was present when we had the wonderful experience of the marriage of our only daughter followed shortly thereafter, by a wedding of the youngest son Jim. Prince also was our only canine companion when I decided to retire from dentistry, not because I didn't enjoy the practice, but since my father had suffered his fatal heart attack at age 46, I had the uneasy feeling that I might suffer a similar fate. To retire at age 57 was a difficult choice, but I really have never regretted doing it. My practice was very ably taken over by Dr. Thomas A Johnston with the unwavering loyal help of Jan Griggs R.N., Lucie Lewin, R.D.H. and Karen Haskell R.D.H. Dr. Tom and Karen have been providing excellent dental care for my old patients for the last 23 years. I was exceedingly blessed to have a wonderful staff for all of those years.

The four children were already out of college, and seemed to be well entrenched in their respective careers, so when I decided to leave dentistry, I was fortunate enough to have one of our patients express interest in taking over from me. Prince One was to become one of the few "Golden Retriever Snow Birds," as we spent six months in sunny Florida, and six months in partially sunny Vermont. This made Gwen, who loves warm weather, very happy and Prince of course, didn't care where he lived as long as we were there. This is a very typical Golden response and reaction.

I think all of our dogs preferred Vermont to Florida, since there were far fewer restrictions on them relative to movement in the environment. When Prince passed in Florida, after his 10 good years, we were first undecided as to whether we would continue the "Golden Years." However, after our arrival back in Vermont for the summer of 1996, without a canine presence, it did not take very long for us to realize that we could not survive dog-less, and so the search was on.

When the twins, as I called them, Prince Too and Angel Princess, arrived from northern Vermont, we were once again back on track. If you think that one Golden can give you a lot of love and pleasure, then you should try two. We had always felt that our dogs were far more content when they had a companion canine to supplement their human owners.

Prince Too and Angel were really prime examples of Velcro as they virtually stuck to each other if Gwen or I were not available. Since we were retired during the entire life span of these two, we seemed to grow closer to them than we had been with any of their predecessors. There was a constant flow of love and appreciation between all of our dogs, but in some ways these last two were special.

We were also blessed to have been involved a little bit with the three Goldens that son John has had, and even though our time with them was limited, it was always enjoyable. This period of time and pleasure with Goldens was enhanced by son John's string of three wonderful dogs of which two are still alive. He started with his orphan dog Tyler, who was his introduction to this wonderful breed, who was followed by the goofy but lovable Parker. "Parky," as we sometimes called him he loved ice cubes, and as soon as we were ready for a cocktail hour, he planted himself in front of the freezer, waiting for you to drop a cube into his eager jaws. He remained a lovable oaf, even through his painful experiences that included two hip surgeries and finally the amputation of his rear leg. His three legged antics always amazed me as he still thinks he has a complete set of underpinnings. I never call him "Tripod" to his face, even if he could never comprehend its meaning. And finally our greyhound like Tally, worlds' fastest dog, is daily making Parker's life a little more bearable as she provides him with the activity that makes him forget his disability. She and Parker again are living proof that Goldens thrive on the love and companionship that are provided by another dog or even better a human of their own.

As I finished writing this story, it has been a little over a year that we have been separated from the tender loving presence of our last Golden, and we have thought many times that we should renew and prolong "My 50 Golden Years," and only time will tell. It would probably not be a mistake however it turns out, but I will be forever grateful for my half century spent with these magnificent examples of "Man's best friend."

MY50GY@aol.com